Soup, Salad
and
Pasta Innovations

Books by Karen Lee with Alaxandra Branyon

SOUP, SALAD AND PASTA INNOVATIONS
CHINESE COOKING SECRETS

Books by Karen Lee

CHINESE COOKING FOR THE AMERICAN KITCHEN

Soup, Salad

and Pasta Innovations

by *Karen Lee*

WRITTEN WITH
Alaxandra Branyon

DOUBLEDAY & COMPANY, INC.
GARDEN CITY, NEW YORK   1987

Illustrations by Lauren Jarrett

DESIGN BY M FRANKLIN-PLYMPTON

Library of Congress Cataloging-in-Publication Data
Lee, Karen.
    Soup, salad and pasta innovations.
    Includes index.
    1. Soups. 2. Salads. 3. Cookery (Macaroni)
I. Branyon, Alaxandra. II. Title.
TX757.L42 1987   641.8′13   86-13573
ISBN: 0-385-19864-7

Acknowledgments

Who do you know who would answer her door at 9 A.M. and dutifully taste seven salad dressings with an assortment of accompanying greens, and give judgment? Going beyond her responsibilities by contributing to the culinary importance of this book as well as its *raison d'être,* she is none other than Alaxandra Branyon, who remains my valued writing collaborator.

To my loyal experimental class who met every Monday night to help me test all the recipes in this book, who gave me the encouragement and motivation to complete this project, thank you.

To Ruth Rothstein, who honed the details until they were perfect as no one else could, as if the book were her child, thank you.

K.L.

Contents

Introduction

What Everyone Likes

A soup, salad, and pasta menu draws people to the table like a magnet. After all, that's what everyone likes to eat. We respond to soups, salads, and pastas with great excitement and satisfaction because we like to feel good before, during, and after dining. As this type of meal can be low in cholesterol, high in fiber, and filled with complex carbohydrates and vegetable proteins, it fits our lighter, healthier way of eating.

These particular recipes adapt to today's lifestyle as they address the cook's dilemma of being rushed and sophisticated, of wanting recipes that are easy to prepare but look and taste hard to make. Many procedures can be done ahead of time and often dishes can be made entirely in advance, refrigerated for several days, or frozen. There are numerous dishes that can be served at room temperature.

You can create your own original, exciting menu from these recipes, and after you enjoy your wonderfully fresh, very special, magnificent soup, salad, or pasta, you, too, will feel both content and energized.

What's for Dinner?

I have added soups, salads, and pasta dishes to my catering menu and teaching schedule, which in the past was totally Chinese. I feel as though I am in semiretirement, as the menus are that much easier to assemble.

Because many of these dishes contain meat, fish, or poultry, it is not necessary to have the official main course that is traditionally expected in an American meal. You can simply serve a soup-salad-pasta three-course nontraditional dinner.

You can also use these dishes individually to fill out your regular menus. Have a soup, salad, or pasta as a first or second course then have your entree such as grilled fish, roast chicken, baked ham, or roast sirloin of beef. And you can let a dish function one way today and another way tomorrow. Serve a hearty soup like Uncle Vanya's Matchstick Soup with a crusty loaf of bread for a whole meal. Tomorrow, when there's only a little left, have it as a first course.

These dishes are appropriate for many eating occasions. Lunch, dinner, large buffet, and "aftermaths." That's when hungry people come over late after some function and you pull out the cold soups, hot soups, room-temperature salads, or pastas.

Many of these recipes are light-eating fare, so you are free to plan any type of dessert you wish. I prefer to keep the dessert on the simple side. Poached pears with a raspberry sauce or baked apples with the addition of a little crème fraîche to deglaze the bottom of the pan in which they were baked. With these menus, I often serve fresh pineapple and berries. Or, if I feel ambitious, a lemon meringue pie. Somehow the citrus provides a clean finish.

When I want to entertain guests and at the same time include myself as a member of the party, I think of the recipes in this book, which for the most part can be prepared before the guests arrive or completed in minimal time afterward. Check the Plan Ahead notes following the recipes for specific instructions. Because you can do almost everything in advance, this is truly a working person's cookbook.

If you're the cook and you want something special at the end of a working day, set aside a Saturday afternoon and make soup or sauce and refrigerate or freeze it. Bear in mind that many of the pasta sauces and some of the soups actually improve in flavor if made ahead several days. Make the dressings for the salads two days in advance (add the garlic just before using).

By doing most of the cooking ahead of time, you can be free to enjoy your family, your guests, and your food. Whether they are prepared for a small family dinner or a large party buffet, let these dishes work together for you.

Taking a Good Idea

Recipes don't just come out of nowhere. In my case, they come from my fifteen years' experience as a teacher of cooking and my travels as a professional cook, during which time I have developed variations of classic dishes and adaptations of old favorite recipes of students and friends.

Even when people give me a recipe, I don't merely type it up. Each dish has to be worked through, tested, and retested. Sometimes I make dishes more elaborate, sometimes I make them less rich. I love to save a few calories without sacrificing anything to flavor. I rely on feedback from my experimental class, all of them hard-core "foodies" with cooking experience and good taste. Ultimately I add my own style.

One major source of ideas for these recipes was the specialty food shops with the zillion-dollar-per-pound take-out dishes. Another was fine restaurants everywhere. Both of these sources rarely have a published recipe to match an exquisite dish, so to re-create the seasonings and the dishes on my own I follow a definite method.

First of all I carry a purse in which I can comfortably fit a small glass jar. Or two. Or three. My forte happens to be taking a good idea and making it into a better one. So, if I am dining out and should happen to taste a brilliant dish or even a good one that I think I can elevate to a higher standard . . . I never finish the dish, but instead I rather surreptitiously fill the jar and return home with it. The next day I try to duplicate it while it is fresh on my mind and palate. Sometimes I am successful right away and other times it takes me several attempts. On occasion I fall short of my expectations.

Other recipes I just developed on my own. How? I go into the kitchen and *potchkeh* around. Sometimes I base a new idea on the ingredients that are in season or in the refrigerator. I have had particular fun with this book by taking Chinese leftovers and turning them into pasta sauces or salads.

In any case, obtaining the very best ingredients is a prerequisite to making memorable dishes. As the late restaurateur Henri Soulé said, "I am very easy to please, as long as you show me the best!" In my culinary journeys, I like to scout around for the local specialties before selecting a menu. Chances are the closer an item is grown to where you are, the fresher it is. Of course there are always exceptions. Raspberries from Chile are very often better than they are on Long Island at the height of the season.

If real cream (not ultrapasteurized) turns you on and plastic tomatoes turn you off, if when you cook you use food and not chemicals, then this book is for you.

Planning It Out

I plan out a soup, salad, pasta menu the same way I would a Chinese dinner.

1. Look carefully at all the recipes you intend to use. Particularly check those ingredients that are capitalized. Buy or make those items on a day when you are not cooking dinner. Things like Hot Sauce, Chicken Stock, Tomato Sauce, and Pesto Base should be at your fingertips so you can assemble a dish or dinner easily.

2. If you are cooking for a large number of people, select one or two soups, three or four salads, one or two pastas. After deciding on the menu, look at all the recipes for any repetition of ingredients. Do these preparations together. For instance, I wash, stem, and process the parsley leaves two bunches at a time in the food processor. I blanch and peel the shallots, then process them altogether. I crush the garlic, remove the peeling, then process. Each ingredient is then placed in a bowl and covered with plastic wrap. You will be jumping around to all the different recipes, working on all of them at once, but in the end this type of organization will save you lots of time.

3. Look over the recipes again and see what can be done a day in advance and do it. At the end of each recipe look under the heading PLAN AHEAD.

4. Set up trays. Dishes that require last-minute attention should have a tray. All the ingredients are placed on the tray, ready to be added to the sauté skillet. This reduces the possibility of error or a forgotten ingredient.

5. Heat the serving dishes. Keep them warm in a 250° oven.

6. Have your pot filled with water ready to boil for the pasta; the chosen sauté skillet ready to go; extra oil, butter, salt, stock, and the pepper mill ready and near the stove for any last-minute adjustments.

7. Place a typed menu on the refrigerator so you can't forget a salad you made the day before.

Being organized cuts down on the anxiety many hostesses feel. The more at ease you feel, the more you and your guests will enjoy your efforts.

What Does It Mean?

Serves 2 to 4:
2, if it's served as a main course;
4, if it's served as a first course.

"Fresh" pasta:
As long as a store makes it fresh, it doesn't have to be homemade.

An ingredient that is capitalized:
There is a recipe elsewhere in the book for the item. Consult the index for its location.

An ingredient that is marked with an asterisk:*
Additional information about this item can be found in the NOTE at the end of the recipe.

Soups

Choosing a Soup

If you want to get your salivary glands going, your gastric juices flowing, and your appetite stimulated, have some soup. A thin, clear soup like Clam and Icicle Radish Soup. A delicate one like French Carrot and Dill Soup. A husky one like Indian Split Pea Soup. Soups are good in any season. A cool Summer Tomato and Yogurt Soup is as greatly appreciated on a warm August night as is a body-warming soup served very hot on a blustery winter evening.

There is a soup to fit whatever your mood. Some people like a soup as the main part of their meal, served with a salad and a crusty loaf of hot bread. Filling this need are such hearty thick soups as Beef Goulash, Uncle Vanya's Matchstick Soup, and Provincial Vegetable Soup with Saffron and Herbs. Other people like soup as a first course. Fresh Asparagus Soup with Knödel makes a wonderful first course with its homemade bread dumplings that are so good they would even be outstanding in a clear consommé, let alone a rich and flavorful asparagus brew. Sour Cream and Zucchini Dill Soup is an excellent choice to serve as a prelude to an elegant meal.

The type of soup you choose should complement the rest of the meal. For instance, try to find contrasts in temperatures and colors. Before a cold dish like Scallop and Caviar Salad, serve a steaming Cranberry Cabbage Soup. If cream is in the soup, that ingredient should not be repeated or at least not featured in the other dinner courses. Nor would you serve a creamy soup if the main course is rich. A soup like Escarole and Pasta Soup, which has no cream in it, would be a good selection. If the main course is broiled or roasted, serve a richer soup like Mushroom and Potato Soup with Crème Fraîche or a creamy one like Sea Nymph Soup.

Choosing a soup. That's what I call a good problem.

Soup, Salad and Pasta Innovations
Making a Great Soup

If people knew how simple the preparation and procedures for making soup are, they wouldn't just order it in restaurants. Not only is it easy to make, it is hard to mess up if you use a good basic stock and carefully selected fresh, quality ingredients.

The key to making a great soup is to start with a good base. That base is a good stock. There is such a thing as stockless soup, made by merely adding boiling water and simmering for an hour or so; however, since soup is after all a liquid food, a rich, savory stock gives you a head start.

A basic soup stock should taste good on its own before even one ingredient is added to enhance its flavor. It will taste good because when you simmer chicken or beef with vegetables and seasonings in water for a long, long time, the much reduced extractives are quite intense. They are not only flavorful but also nourishing.

Because I like to simmer stock up to twelve hours, I choose a time to make it when I'm going to be home all day. I make it in a large quantity and freeze it so that I can have a soup's foundation at my fingertips.

Other than stocking your freezer with stock, you will need mostly ordinary, readily available ingredients for your soup larder. Have on hand such staples as salt, fresh black pepper, sugar, flour, oil, and a variety of dried herbs. You'll need a dairy product here and there and possibly some canned tomatoes. If you feel creative, you can give some of the hearty soups a more intense flavor by adding the defatted drippings from a roast right into the simmering pot.

As for fresh ingredients, keep in mind that a good soup will bring out their flavor and therefore your goal should be to search for the very best young local fresh vegetables and herbs.

It wouldn't hurt to keep around a potato, some raw rice, and dried beans, all of which can be used to thicken a soup, as can a roux. People have been using roux as a thickening agent for a long time. Flour browned slowly in fat was described in a fifteenth-century manuscript. The reason you blend butter with flour over low heat is that slow cooking eliminates the flour taste. When using this thickening method, it is a good idea to heat the stock in a separate saucepan before adding it to the roux. This step will save you approximately ten minutes of time waiting for the stock to come to a simmer.

From time to time you'll need an egg and a little cream to thicken a soup. This is a typical French method in which an egg yolk and a small quantity of cream are beaten together with a wooden spoon in a small bowl. Some of the simmering soup is then added to this mixture, which introduces heat slowly to the egg yolk and prevents it from curdling when it is poured into the soup. Add this thickener at the last moment before serving the soup. Leftover quantities of soup should be rewarmed over very low heat the following day lest the egg yolk curdle.

Soup Equipment

You don't need a whole array of equipment to make soups—a few enamel saucepans, at least three different sizes, up to six to eight quarts. Choose a brand that is heavy-gauged. For making stock, a giant stainless-steel stockpot is your best choice—the largest one you can store.

I have found that the old-fashioned piece of kitchen equipment called the food mill is invaluable when it comes to blending soups. Especially for vegetable-based soup, it is far better than the processor, as it leaves a little texture.

Because soups are ideal for freezing, you will need wide-mouthed glass jars. Remember to allow for expansion and only fill the container two-thirds full. Soups can be stored in the freezer for several months.

Soups made one to two days ahead of when you plan to serve them can be refrigerated. You will need the same wide-mouthed glass jars you use for freezing. How fresh your stock is will determine how long you can safely refrigerate your soup. If the stock has been frozen, the soup can be kept in the refrigerator for two days; if the stock is fresh, the soup can be refrigerated for four days.

Chicken Stock

I must confess I never follow a recipe for stock. Not even my own recipe. I save bones from the carcasses of poultry I have boned in classes and for catering assignments. I freeze them, and when the freezer door will not close, I know it is time to make stock. I save parts because it just seems unnecessarily extravagant to cook a chicken you are going to throw away. I fill the stockpot with as many carcasses, necks, backs, and giblets as I have, plus one pound of chicken feet to give it a gelatinous quality. I then add seasonings and water to cover by a few inches. Because I make a large quantity at a time, I simmer it 12 hours. If you are only making a few quarts, a 12-hour simmering period would cause the entire stock to evaporate. To achieve a good full flavor, however, stock should simmer at least 6 hours.

When your stock has cooled, taste it. If it is weak, simmer it over the lowest possible heat for another few hours or until it has reduced by a third or more. Keep in mind that stock should never be covered while it is simmering or while it is cooling in the refrigerator lest it turn sour.

The difference between using a can or cube of commercially manufactured stock and a homemade one is dramatic in terms of the flavor of the finished dish. Another major advantage of homemade stock is that you can avoid the high salt content of commercially made stock. *I never add salt when making stock.* Too much salt can wreck a dish. If you have to use a commercially made stock, taste before you add any salt. Also for those who are allergic to MSG, many canned stocks contain this ingredient. Read the label.

**5 pounds chicken parts such
  as necks, backs, and giblets***
**1 pound chicken feet, toenails
  trimmed (optional)**
2–3 medium-size leeks
10 whole peppercorns
1 bay leaf

Several sprigs of parsley
**1 carrot, scrubbed but not
  peeled**
**1 piece parsley root, scrubbed
  but not peeled (optional)**
**Thick piece of celery heart or
  celery root, peeled**

Yield approximately 2 quarts

1. Rinse the chicken parts and the chicken feet under cold running water. Place in an 8-quart or bigger stockpot. Add water to cover by a few inches, about 4 quarts. Bring to a boil over high heat. With a fine mesh skimmer, remove the scum as it rises to the top. This process will take about 10 minutes.

2. Remove the root end of the leeks, then split the leeks in half lengthwise all the way through. Place them under forcefully running warm water

to remove all traces of sand. Then cut the green part only into 2-inch pieces (reserve the white part for use in other recipes). The yield should be 4 cups cut leeks.

3. Turn the heat to low. Add the leeks, peppercorns, bay leaf, parsley, carrot, parsley root, and celery heart. Simmer the stock uncovered for 4 to 6 hours.

4. Strain the stock through a colander set over a stainless-steel bowl; discard the chicken and all the vegetables. Strain the stock one more time through a fine mesh sieve or line a strainer with several layers of cheese-cloth that have been rinsed and wrung dry. Refrigerate the stock *uncovered*. To avoid its becoming sour, do not cover the stock until it has thoroughly cooled. Once it has cooled and the fat has solidified, remove the fat, then refrigerate or freeze in small jars.

PLAN AHEAD

Homemade stock will keep for about 1 week in the refrigerator (longer if it is brought to a simmer every other day, again with no cover). Any kind of stock can be frozen in small quantities, preferably in glass jars. Allow for expansion by filling the jar to two thirds of capacity. It can also be frozen in ice-cube trays, after which the frozen stock cubes can be placed in a glass jar or plastic bag.

*NOTE

If you want to make veal stock, you can substitute an equal quantity of veal for the chicken. Use a combination of meat and bones from the neck and shank. Follow the same recipe.

This stock can be used in any of the following recipes that call for chicken stock. If you substitute a commercially made brand for home-made, omit the salt from the soup or sauce recipe as the stock will already be well salted.

Beef Stock

2 pounds beef*
6–8 pounds marrowbones, cut
in 2 to 3-inch lengths
2 carrots, scrubbed but not
peeled
1 large onion, peeled and
quartered
1 cup diced celery root,
peeled*
1 small green bell pepper,
split, seeds and membrane
removed

1 cup canned Italian tomatoes
(measured with their juice)
or 1/2 pound well-ripened
fresh tomatoes, diced
1 potato, scrubbed and
quartered
Several sprigs of parsley
10 whole black peppercorns

Yield 1 gallon

1. Preheat the oven to 400°. Place the beef and the marrowbones in a roasting pan. Roast for about 40 minutes or until they have browned.

2. Place the beef and the bones in a large enamel or stainless-steel stockpot. Do not wash the roasting pan. Cover the beef and bones with cold water by several inches. Bring to a boil. Remove the scum with a fine mesh sieve. This will take about 10 minutes. Turn the heat to low.

3. While the stock is coming to a boil, deglaze the roasting pan in which the meat and bones were roasted. To do this, pour out any fat from the roasting pan. Add about 2 cups of water, then place the pan over high heat. Stir with a wooden spoon to incorporate all the coagulated juices into the water. Pour this deglazing liquid into the stockpot from which the scum has been removed.

4. Add the remaining ingredients and simmer for 3 to 4 hours or until the meat is fork tender. Never let it boil.

5. Remove the meat from the simmering stock. Allow the stock to simmer another 6 to 8 hours.

6. Strain the stock, first through a colander, and then through a sieve lined with cheesecloth that has been rinsed and squeezed dry.

Refrigerate *uncovered* until the fat congeals. Remove the fat. Refrigerate or freeze in glass jars, filled to two thirds of capacity.

PLAN AHEAD

Homemade beef stock will keep for about a week in the refrigerator, or it can be frozen indefinitely. For recipes requiring just a few tablespoons of stock, freeze a portion of the stock in ice-cube containers. When the cubes have formed, place in a plastic bag and return to the freezer.

*NOTE

The 2 pounds of beef can be lean brisket, chicken steak, short ribs, or shin. For soup recipes such as Uncle Vanya's Matchstick Soup, which require boiled beef, the preferred cut of beef is lean brisket or chicken steak.

For the celery root, you can substitute an equal amount of celery.

This stock can be used in any of the following recipes that call for beef stock. If you substitute a commercially made brand for homemade, omit the salt from the soup or sauce recipe as the stock will already be well salted.

Glace de Viande

Glace de viande means a reduction of defatted beef stock or stock of mixed meats and poultry. Any type of stock, however, can be concentrated to its very essence. When you use a reduced stock in your cooking, it's like getting a head start in a race. With a tablespoon of Glace de Viande, you are immediately enhancing the flavor of sauces, stews, and soups.

2 quarts defatted and salt-free homemade beef, veal, or chicken stock (or a combination)

Place the stock in a saucepan and reduce over the lowest possible heat until 1 cup remains. Pour small quantities of the reduced stock into glass jars and refrigerate or freeze. This reduced stock, or Glace de Viande, can be stored in the refrigerator for 1 week or in the freezer indefinitely.

Fresh Asparagus Soup with Knödel

Whoever said neighbors don't talk to each other in New York City? I met Mrs. Russo eighteen years ago. She is a fabulous Viennese cook who specializes in soups. Her mother was Hungarian, her father was Yugoslavian, and she was born in Vienna in 1913. Brought up on haute cuisine, she proudly says, "My understanding of good food comes from home." The six recipes that follow were generously taught to me by Mrs. Russo. They are all original old family recipes that have never before been published, and are mostly Viennese soups taught to her by her mother.

Of all the wonderful soups Mrs. Russo taught me, this fabulous spring season soup happens to be my favorite. The most important thing to remember is that the asparagus must taste wonderful on their own for the soup to be great. I recommend steaming one asparagus and eating it without salt or butter. If it passes the test, then use the rest for this soup.

KNÖDEL (DUMPLINGS)
1/3 cup bread crumbs to be made from French bread*
1 egg
1 tablespoon corn oil
2 teaspoons chopped parsley
1/2 teaspoon salt

1 pound fresh asparagus
3 tablespoons butter

2 tablespoons flour
1/2 cup chopped parsley
Freshly ground black pepper (10 turns of the mill)
3 cups Chicken Stock

1 egg yolk at room temperature
3 tablespoons crème fraîche at room temperature*

Serves 4–6

1. *To make the bread crumbs:* Preheat the oven to 250°. Cut white French bread into cubes. Place the cubes on a cookie sheet and bake for about 45 minutes or until they are well dried out. Allow to cool. Place in a food processor and blend.

2. *To make the knödel:* Place 1 egg in a bowl and beat with a fork. Add the corn oil, the 2 teaspoons parsley, the 1/2 teaspoon salt, and continue to beat with a fork until all the ingredients are well combined. Add the bread crumbs and continue to beat another minute with the fork. Refrigerate the mixture for at least 1 hour.

3. *To make the soup:* While the mixture is in the refrigerator, cut off and discard approximately 2 inches from the base of each asparagus. Peel the asparagus (do not peel the tip end). Slant-cut 2 cups of asparagus into 2-inch pieces. Set aside.

4. In a stainless-steel or enamel 1 1/2 to 2-quart saucepan, melt the

butter over a low heat. Add the flour and stir rapidly with a wooden spoon to make a loose roux. Simmer the roux for about 1 minute. Add the parsley, continuing to stir another 2 minutes. Add the asparagus, pepper, and chicken stock. Turn the heat to high. Bring the soup to a simmer, stirring in a figure-8 motion. Turn the heat to low. Cover and simmer the soup for 15 to 20 minutes.

5. Remove the bread-crumb mixture from the refrigerator. With wet hands, form the mixture into very small balls (⅓ the size of walnuts). Add to the simmering soup and gently cook, uncovered, for 10 minutes. Turn off the heat.

6. In a separate bowl, mix the egg yolk and crème fraîche together. To prevent the egg yolk from curdling, pour ¼ cup hot soup into this mixture and stir well. Add the mixture to the soup, stirring constantly in a figure-8 motion to reach the center of the saucepan. Serve immediately.

PLAN AHEAD

This soup can be prepared early in the day, but be careful when you are rewarming it. Make sure you rewarm it over a very low heat so the egg yolk does not curdle, and don't let the soup come to a boil after it simmers.

*NOTE

The amount of bread crumbs in the knödel depends on the size of the egg. More bread crumbs are needed with a larger egg. I prefer homemade bread crumbs but commercially made ones are available. Store your homemade bread crumbs in a covered glass jar. They will keep for 2 months in the refrigerator.

For the crème fraîche, an equal amount of heavy cream can be substituted.

Sweet Pea Soup with Spätzle

This is a typical seasonal Viennese soup. Spätzle are irregular-shaped dumplings. Fresh peas really make the difference, but frozen will do in a pinch. Never canned. To quote Mrs. Russo's soup philosophy, "Soups should never boil, only simmer slowly to get all the flavor out of the vegetables. The smaller the flame, the better the soup."

SPÄTZLE
1 egg
1 scant tablespoon corn oil
1/2 teaspoon salt
Freshly ground black pepper
  (8 turns of the mill)
1 teaspoon chopped parsley
3–4 tablespoons flour

4 cups Chicken Stock

3 tablespoons butter
2 tablespoons flour
1/2 cup chopped parsley
2 cups shelled fresh peas or
  frozen peas
Freshly ground black pepper
  (10 turns of the mill)
1 teaspoon sugar

Serves 4–6

1. *To make the spätzle:* Place the egg in a bowl and beat with a fork. Add the oil, salt, pepper, and parsley; continue to beat with a fork until all the ingredients are well combined. Add the 3–4 tablespoons flour a little at a time, continuing to beat with the fork. The amount of flour will depend on the size of the egg. The dumpling mixture should have a consistency thicker than pancake batter. Refrigerate the spätzle for 20 minutes or longer.

2. *To make the soup:* In a saucepan, bring the chicken stock to a simmer over low heat. Do not cover.

3. In another saucepan (1 1/2 to 2 quarts), melt the butter over low heat. Add the 2 tablespoons flour and stir rapidly with a wooden spoon to make a loose roux. Simmer the roux for about 1 minute. Add the parsley to the roux, continuing to stir another minute. Add the peas and pepper; continue to stir another 2 minutes.

4. Add the heated stock all at once, then the sugar. Bring to a simmer over high heat, stirring in a figure-8 motion with a wooden spoon (to reach the center of the saucepan). Turn the heat to low and simmer covered for 10 minutes if frozen peas, 20 minutes if fresh.

5. Add the spätzle to the simmering soup a little at a time with a teaspoon: place the teaspoon in the dumpling mixture, then push the spätzle off the teaspoon into the soup with your index finger. Repeat as many times as needed, working quickly until all the dumpling mixture has been used. Simmer uncovered for another 15 minutes over very low heat. Serve piping hot.

Sour Cream and Zucchini Dill Soup

When I asked Mrs. Russo how she created this dish, she told me, "It started as a vegetable dish, then I decided to turn it into a soup. Dill goes well with sour cream and zucchini goes well with dill. The whole combination is perfect. I know what goes with what."

3 tablespoons butter
2 tablespoons flour
1/2 cup minced fresh dill
3 tablespoons sugar
Salt to taste
Freshly ground black pepper
  (10 turns of the mill)

2 tablespoons lemon juice
1 cup sour cream
4 cups sliced unpeeled
  zucchini in thin rounds
4 cups Chicken Stock

Serves 4–6

1. In an enamel or stainless-steel 3 to 4-quart saucepan or a 12-inch sauté skillet, melt the butter over low heat. Add the flour and stir with a wooden spoon to make a roux. Continue to stir for about 1 minute. Add the dill and the sugar; stir another minute. Add the salt, pepper, and lemon juice. Turn the heat to medium. Add the sour cream and the zucchini. Stir a few minutes. Cover and simmer 25 minutes over the lowest possible heat. Stir occasionally.

2. When the 25 minutes are up, bring the chicken stock to a simmer in a separate saucepan. Add the heated chicken stock to the pan containing the zucchini-and-sour-cream mixture. Continue to cook another 5 minutes over low heat, stirring almost constantly.

3. Allow the soup to cool, then purée in a food processor or pass through the smallest opening on a food mill.

This soup can be served cold or hot.

PLAN AHEAD
This soup keeps very well in the refrigerator for up to 5 days. It may also be frozen.

Beef Goulash Soup

This is also a typical Viennese soup. It is made with the tail of the filet, which is better than stew meat because it takes a shorter time to cook and doesn't get stringy when you reheat it.

2 tablespoons butter	1/4 pound fresh mushrooms, sliced
2 tablespoons corn oil	
1 tablespoon sweet Hungarian paprika*	2 tablespoons chopped parsley
	3 cups peeled and cubed potatoes
4 cups sliced Spanish onions	
1 pound filet mignon tail, in 1/2-inch cubes	1 teaspoon salt
	1 cup water
Freshly ground black pepper (20 turns of the mill)	1 cup Chicken Stock
	2 cups Beef Stock
1 tablespoon minced garlic	1 cup sour cream

Serves 4–6

1. In a 12-inch sauté skillet, heat the butter with 1 tablespoon of the corn oil until the butter melts. Add the paprika and the onions; sauté over medium heat for about 10 minutes or until the onions start to brown.

2. While the onions are sautéing, place an iron skillet over high heat until it smokes. Add the remaining tablespoon corn oil and heat until very hot. Add the beef cubes and sauté a few minutes or until they have browned. Add the pepper. Turn off the heat. Do not wash this skillet.

3. To the skillet containing the onions, add the garlic and sauté about 1 minute. Add the mushrooms, parsley, the browned beef, potatoes, and salt.

4. Deglaze the iron skillet with 1 cup water. Add the deglazing liquid, the 1 cup chicken stock and 2 cups beef stock to the soup. Turn the heat to high and bring the soup to a simmer. Turn the heat to low. Cover and simmer for about 1 hour, stirring occasionally.

5. Serve piping hot with sour cream on the side.

PLAN AHEAD

Beef Goulash Soup lasts for several days in the refrigerator. It also freezes well.

*NOTE

Taste the paprika before using. It should be sweet. If it is not, reduce the quantity to 1 teaspoon.

Mushroom and Potato Soup
with Crème Fraîche

This is Mrs. Russo's Viennese home-style soup. She said, "We came home every day for lunch: soup, meat, vegetable, and cake. In the evening we had a sandwich or whatever there was left. We had no refrigerator. Everything was bought fresh every day. The milk was portioned out in a pail and the last of it was finished off at night."

3 tablespoons butter
2 tablespoons flour
1 cup sliced Spanish onions
1 cup chopped parsley
3/4 pound fresh mushrooms, cut in half circles
3/4 pound potatoes, peeled and cut in half circles

3 cups Chicken Stock
1 teaspoon salt
Freshly ground black pepper (20 turns of the mill)
1/2 cup crème fraîche*

Serves 6–8

1. In a 2-quart saucepan, heat the butter until it foams. Add the flour and stir constantly for a few minutes or until the butter and flour have been well combined over low heat.

2. Add the onions and sauté 5 minutes or until slightly brown. Add the parsley and continue to sauté about 2 minutes. Add the mushrooms and sauté another 2 minutes. Add the potatoes, along with the chicken stock, salt, and pepper. Turn the heat to high and bring to a simmer. Turn the heat to low. Cover and simmer 1 hour or until the potatoes are soft, stirring occasionally.

3. Remove the cover and add the crème fraîche, stirring until well combined. Serve piping hot.

PLAN AHEAD
Mushroom and Potato Soup with Crème Fraîche can be stored in the refrigerator for several days or can be frozen.

*NOTE
For the crème fraîche you can substitute 1/4 cup heavy cream and 1/4 cup sour cream.

Cranberry Cabbage Soup

This is Mrs. Russo's version of Viennese classic cabbage soup.

3 tablespoons butter
2 tablespoons flour
2 tablespoons sugar
1/4 cup apple cider vinegar
11/4 cups water
1 teaspoon salt
Freshly ground black pepper
  (30 turns of the mill)

1 medium apple, peeled and
  diced
8 cups shredded red cabbage
4 cups Chicken Stock
1 16-ounce can whole
  cranberry sauce
1 cup sour cream

Serves 10–12

1. In a large saucepan heat the butter until it foams. Add the flour and the sugar, stirring over low heat about 5 minutes or until the sugar caramelizes. Be careful not to let it get too brown. Turn off the heat. Add the vinegar and 1/4 cup of the water. Stir in a figure-8 motion until all the ingredients are well combined.

2. Turn the heat to low. Add the salt, pepper, and diced apple; continue to cook about 2 minutes. Add the cabbage and stir well. Add the remaining 1 cup of water, along with 1 cup of the chicken stock. Turn the heat to high and bring the soup to a simmer. Then turn the heat to low, cover, and simmer 15 minutes. Remove the cover, add 3 more cups of the chicken stock, along with the cranberry sauce, stirring well to combine all the ingredients. Cover and simmer another 11/2 hours, stirring occasionally.

3. Serve piping hot with sour cream on the side.

PLAN AHEAD

Cranberry Cabbage Soup lasts for at least 5 days in the refrigerator. If desired, it can be frozen.

Zucchini Almond Soup

One evening when I was dining at Café La Fraise in Hanover, New Hampshire, with my son Todd, we started off our meal with a lovely soup, the recipe for which the owners were kind enough to share with me. Now I can happily share this adapted version with you.

1 cup blanched whole
  almonds
2 tablespoons butter
1 cup chopped onions
3 medium-size unpeeled
  zucchini, scrubbed and
  sliced (about 5 1/2 cups)
4 cups Chicken Stock
1/2 cup heavy cream

1/2 cup milk
1 tablespoon brown sugar
1 tablespoon almond liqueur
1/4 teaspoon nutmeg
1/4 teaspoon cinnamon
Salt to taste
Freshly ground white pepper
  (10 turns of the mill)

Serves 4–6

1. Preheat the oven to 325°. Place the almonds on a cookie sheet and roast for 15 to 20 minutes or until golden brown. Allow almonds to cool, then pulverize them.

2. In a 3-quart saucepan heat the butter until it foams. Add the onions and sauté over medium heat for 5 minutes or until they start to brown. Add the zucchini. Stirring often, sauté for 5 minutes or until the zucchini is barely tender. Add the chicken stock, bring to a simmer, and cook uncovered over low heat for 20 minutes.

3. Add the ground almonds and simmer another 10 minutes.

4. Add the cream, milk, brown sugar, almond liqueur, nutmeg, cinnamon, salt, and pepper. Stir briefly, then turn off the heat.

5. Strain the soup and reserve the liquid. Add the solids to the food processor and purée until smooth. Return the purée along with the reserved soup liquid to the saucepan. Bring the soup back to simmer, stirring occasionally in a figure-8 motion. Serve piping hot.

PLAN AHEAD
  Zucchini Almond Soup can be prepared several days in advance.

Egyptian Chick-pea Soup

I developed and tested all the recipes in this book with my experimental class. One lucky day a member of the class opened up the treasure chest of soup recipes she has been collecting for decades and shared them with me. Her name is Susan Coates and she makes a great bowl of soup. This recipe and those on pages 26–30 and page 32 are from her collection. Certain recipes were so popular among the students that they would jokingly say, "I think this one should be tested again." Besides being delicious, this soup is also extremely healthful as it provides vegetable protein. The combination of the chick-peas with rice creates a complete protein.

3/4 cup dried chick-peas*
11/2 cups water
1 16-ounce can tomatoes
  (measured with their juice)
2 tablespoons butter
1 cup chopped Spanish onions
1/2 cup diced celery
1/2 cup diced carrots,
  scrubbed but not peeled
3 cloves garlic, minced
5 cups Chicken Stock
Salt to taste
Freshly ground black pepper
  (20 turns of the mill)

1 bay leaf
1 teaspoon cumin
2 tablespoons chopped parsley
1/2 cup raw rice, rinsed and
  drained

GARNISH
Lemon wedges
Chopped cilantro leaves*

1/2 cup grated Parmesan
  cheese

Serves 6–8

1. Place the chick-peas in a bowl and cover with cold water. Cover the bowl and let them soak for 10 hours. Drain the chick-peas. Place them in a small-size saucepan with a tight-fitting cover. Add the 11/2 cups water. Bring to a boil over high heat, then turn the heat to low. Stir briefly, then cover and simmer over low heat until the chick-peas are tender and all the water has evaporated, approximately 1 to 11/4 hours. Remove the chick-peas from the saucepan and allow to cool. You should have about 13/4 cups cooked chick-peas.

2. Pass the tomatoes through a food mill into a bowl. Reserve the puréed tomatoes with their juice; discard the seeds.

3. In a large saucepan, heat the butter until it foams. Add the onions and cook until they are translucent. Add the celery and carrots and cook until they have softened. Add the garlic and cook until it is slightly golden.

Add the chicken stock. Turn the heat to high until the stock comes to a simmer. Then add the salt, pepper, bay leaf, puréed tomatoes, cumin, parsley, and rice.

When the soup comes to a simmer, turn the heat to low. Cover and cook for about 1/2 hour, stirring occasionally.

4. Add the chick-peas to the soup and simmer 1/2 hour more. Remove the bay leaf. Serve the soup piping hot. Garnish with lemon wedges and cilantro. Sprinkle the Parmesan cheese on top.

PLAN AHEAD

Without the garnish and Parmesan, the entire soup can be prepared several days in advance. It also freezes well.

*NOTE

As a shortcut to this soup, you can use one 16-ounce can of chick-peas. Add them and their liquid in step 4.

Cilantro is also known as Chinese parsley or fresh coriander.

Indian Split Pea Soup

The combination of an old and reliable ingredient, split green peas, with the surprise of Indian spices, topped with sautéed onions as a garnish, makes this soup outstanding. I like to add a cup of diced smoked country ham during the last half hour of cooking, but this is an optional step. If you are using ham in the soup, it may not be necessary to add salt.

½ pound split green peas
2 cups water
2 cups canned Italian tomatoes (measured with their juice)
5 cups Chicken Stock
2 cups diced onions
1 clove garlic, minced
1 teaspoon minced ginger
½ teaspoon cardamom
1 teaspoon turmeric

1 teaspoon cumin
Salt to taste
Freshly ground black pepper (20 turns of the mill)

GARNISH
2 tablespoons butter
2 cups sliced onions
Chopped cilantro leaves*

Serves 6–8

1. Rinse the split peas and drain. Pick over them to remove any foreign matter. Place the peas in a large saucepan. Cover with the water. Bring to a boil. Remove from the heat. Cover and allow to sit 1 hour.

2. Pass the tomatoes through a food mill into a bowl. Reserve the puréed tomatoes with their juice; discard the seeds.

3. Add the following to the saucepan containing the split peas: the chicken stock, diced onions, puréed tomatoes and their juice, garlic, ginger, cardamom, turmeric, cumin, salt, and pepper.

Bring the soup to a simmer over high heat. Then turn the heat to low, cover, and simmer 2 to 3 hours or until the peas become creamy. Every 20 minutes or so, check to see that the soup is not cooking too fast and that the peas do not scorch.

4. Place an iron skillet over high heat for about 1 minute. Add the butter. Turn the heat to low. When the butter foams, add the sliced onions. Turn the heat to medium and sauté the onions until they are dark brown.

Serve Indian Split Pea Soup piping hot. Garnish each serving with sautéed onions and cilantro.

PLAN AHEAD

The entire soup can be prepared ahead and will last in the refrigerator for at least 5 days. It also freezes well.

Sautéed onions can be cooked several hours in advance and left uncovered in the iron skillet.

*NOTE

Cilantro is also known as Chinese parsley or fresh coriander.

Swedish Yellow Pea Soup

This rich, flavorful soup makes a hearty winter meal. It gives you so much and demands so little of your time.

1 pound smoked pork butt, trimmed and cut into 1-inch cubes	4 cups salt-free Chicken Stock*
4 cups water	1 cup chopped onions
2 cups dried yellow split peas (1 pound)	Freshly ground black pepper (20 turns of the mill)
	1/2 teaspoon dried marjoram

Serves 6–8

1. Place the pork-butt cubes and water in a medium to large-size saucepan. Bring to a boil. Cover, turn the heat to low, and simmer 2 hours.
2. Add the peas, chicken stock, onions, pepper, and marjoram. Bring to a simmer over high heat, then turn the heat to low. Cover and simmer 2 hours. Check every 20 minutes to make sure that the peas don't scorch. Stir occasionally. Add more chicken stock if the soup becomes too thick. Cook the soup until it is creamy. Serve piping hot.

PLAN AHEAD

The entire soup can be prepared several days in advance. It freezes very well.

*NOTE

You must make your own homemade Chicken Stock for Swedish Yellow Pea Soup because it is imperative that the soup be cooked in a salt-free chicken stock, or else the pork butt will render the soup too salty.

Soup, Salad and Pasta Innovations
Summer Tomato and Yogurt Soup

This recipe and those on pages 30 and 32 will give an exciting and original start to your summer meals.

6 medium, well-ripened tomatoes *or* 3 cups canned Italian tomatoes (measured with their juice)	1/4 cup olive oil*
	1 tablespoon flour
	1 tablespoon tomato paste
	1 teaspoon sugar
2 tablespoons butter	Freshly ground black pepper (20 turns of the mill)
1 1/2 cups chopped Spanish onions	Salt to taste
2 cloves garlic, minced	1 cup plain yogurt
1 quart Chicken Stock	15 basil leaves, chopped*

Serves 6–8

1. Bring a large saucepan of water to a rolling boil. Blanch the tomatoes one at a time for a few seconds. Remove the skin and discard. Discard the seeds, then chop the tomatoes and reserve. If you are using canned tomatoes, pass the tomatoes through a food mill into a bowl. Reserve the puréed tomatoes with their juice; discard the seeds.

2. In a medium-size saucepan, melt the butter until it foams. Sauté the onions over medium heat for about 5 minutes or until they are golden. Add the garlic and continue to sauté for another minute or two or until the garlic begins to turn light brown.

3. While the onions are sautéing, heat the chicken stock in a separate saucepan.

4. Add the olive oil to the saucepan containing the onions and garlic and heat for a few seconds. Then add the flour and stir with a wooden spoon for about 2 minutes. Add the heated chicken stock and stir well in a figure-8 motion to reach the center of the saucepan.

5. Add the tomato paste, sugar, pepper, and salt. Stir a few seconds, then add the tomatoes. If using fresh tomatoes, simmer the soup about 20 minutes. If using canned tomatoes, simmer the soup 30 minutes.

6. Turn off the heat. Stir in the yogurt and basil leaves. Whisk the soup until it is well blended. Refrigerate until ready to serve. Serve chilled.

PLAN AHEAD

This soup can be prepared a day in advance and refrigerated. Any leftover portion should be served during the next 2 days.

*NOTE

For the basil, you can substitute 1 tablespoon Pesto Base. Preferably use fresh Pesto Base rather than frozen. Use only 2 tablespoons olive oil if you are substituting Pesto Base.

Escarole and Pasta Soup

This speedy, nourishing, and satisfying soup makes a nice addition to anyone's repertoire. It's the kind of soup you would expect to be served if you were a guest in an Italian home. It is a light and interesting beginning to an Italian, French, or American meal.

1 pound fresh escarole
1/2 cup butter
1 cup chopped onions
2 cloves garlic, minced
4 cups Chicken Stock
1/2 cup dried pasta, preferably
cappelletti

Salt to taste
Freshly ground black pepper
(20 turns of the mill)
1/3 cup grated Parmesan
cheese

Serves 4–6

1. Separate and wash the escarole leaves; spin-dry. Cut the leaves into approximately 1-inch pieces.
2. In a large pot melt the butter until it foams. Add the onions and sauté about 5 minutes or until they start to turn light brown. Add the garlic and continue to sauté until it turns slightly golden. Add the escarole pieces and sauté 2–3 minutes, stirring constantly.
3. Add the chicken stock. Bring to a simmer over high heat. Add the pasta. Bring to a simmer again. Cover, turn the heat to low, and simmer another 10 minutes or until the pasta is tender but firm. Add salt and pepper. Serve piping hot. Sprinkle the Parmesan cheese on top.

PLAN AHEAD
   The entire soup can be prepared several hours in advance. If you decide to make the soup in advance, then the pasta should be undercooked, so that when it is reheated it will not be overcooked.

Cold Raspberry Soup

1/2 cup sugar
1 stick cinnamon
1 1/2 cups plus 2 tablespoons
  water

2 cups raspberries
1 tablespoon arrowroot*
1/4 cup heavy cream
1/3 cup dry red wine

Serves 3–4

1. In a medium-size saucepan, combine the sugar, the cinnamon stick, and the 1 1/2 cups water. Bring to a boil over high heat. Turn the heat to low and simmer 10 minutes. Add the raspberries and simmer another 5 minutes.

2. In a small cup, dissolve the arrowroot in the 2 tablespoons cold water. Add this mixture to the simmering soup. Stir in a figure-8 motion to reach the center of the saucepan for about 2 minutes or until the soup is clear. Pour the soup into a glass bowl. Cover and chill for at least 2 hours or overnight.

3. Before eating, take out the cinnamon. Stir in the cream and the red wine. Combine well. Serve cold.

PLAN AHEAD

The entire soup can be prepared early in the day and refrigerated.

*NOTE

For the arrowroot you can substitute cornstarch.

Honeydew Melon
and Avocado Soup

I met Chef Gregory on a trip to China in the summer of 1979. We were traveling with a group of food editors and writers. He is a generous, fun-loving man who is a corporate executive chef. A few years after the trip, we catered together in Columbus, Ohio. It was a fund-raising event for the Boy Scouts, a dinner for three hundred people. Chef Gregory was scaling up the quantities of his dishes by throwing in more until he felt the right consistency, and I was carefully multiplying with my calculator. He nicknamed me R2D2!

One of the cold soups on the menu was this simple and tasty Honeydew Melon and Avocado Soup created by Chef Gregory. It's a great, light, wonderful beginning to meals of many different origins. Make it in the summer or fall when perfectly ripened honeydew melons are in season.

1 small-size, well-ripened honeydew melon
1 medium-size, well-ripened avocado

4 tablespoons fresh lime juice
2 tablespoons orange-flavored liqueur, such as Triple Sec or Grand Marnier

Serves 6

1. Split the melon. Scoop out and discard the seeds. Scoop out the fruit. You should have about 3 cups, with the juice.
2. Cut the avocado in half, discard the pit, and scoop out the meat.
3. Place the avocado and the honeydew melon, along with the lime juice and the liqueur, in the container of a food processor or blender. Process until smooth. Serve chilled.

PLAN AHEAD
Honeydew Melon and Avocado Soup can be made early in the day.

Soup, Salad and Pasta Innovations

Chilled Cream of Cucumber and Yogurt Soup

2 medium-size cucumbers
2 tablespoons butter
1/2 cup chopped onions
2 cups Chicken Stock
Salt to taste
Freshly ground white pepper
   (20 turns of the mill)
1/4 teaspoon sweet paprika

1 teaspoon Dijon mustard
1/4 teaspoon turmeric
1/2 cup plain yogurt
1/2 cup sour cream

GARNISH
Watercress leaves

Serves 4–6

1. Peel the cucumbers, then cut them in half lengthwise. Using a spoon, scoop out the seeds. Grate the cucumber on the coarsest side of the grater. The yield should be about 2 cups.

2. In a medium-size saucepan, heat the butter until it foams. Add the onions and cook over low heat for about 2 to 3 minutes or until they are transparent. Add the grated cucumber and sauté briefly. Add the chicken stock. Bring the soup to a simmer, then cook over low heat until the cucumbers are transparent. This should take about 3 to 5 minutes.

3. Add the salt, pepper, paprika, mustard, and turmeric. Stir in a figure-8 motion to reach the center of the saucepan. Simmer the soup another few minutes until all the seasonings have been well combined. Add the yogurt and sour cream. Continue to stir until mixed well.

4. Refrigerate the soup until it has thoroughly cooled. When ready to serve, garnish with watercress leaves.

PLAN AHEAD

The entire soup can be prepared several days in advance and refrigerated.

Peasant Bean and Sausage Soup

1 cup dried white navy beans
4 cups Chicken Stock
1 link smoked Polish sausage,
    about 4–5 ounces, sliced in
    thin rounds
2 cups chopped onions
2 cups shredded white
    cabbage

1/2 cup sliced carrots,
    scrubbed but not peeled
1/4 teaspoon cumin
Freshly ground black pepper
    (20 turns of the mill)

GARNISH
1/4 cup chopped parsley

Serves 4–6

1. Place the dried beans in a bowl and completely cover them with cold or room-temperature water. Let them soak overnight. Rinse and drain the beans. Place them in a saucepan and cover with cold water by 1 inch. Bring the beans to a moderate boil on top of the stove. Turn the heat to low and simmer until tender, about 1 hour.

2. Place the beans and all their liquid in a large saucepan, along with the chicken stock, sausage, onions, cabbage, carrots, cumin, and pepper. Bring to a simmer over high heat. Turn the heat to low. Cover and simmer at least 1 hour or until quite thick. The soup should be served piping hot, garnished with chopped parsley.

PLAN AHEAD

This soup can be made in advance and will last several days in the refrigerator. It also freezes well.

Provincial Vegetable Soup
with Saffron and Herbs

This is a monumental soup, one which I have worked on for years. It is my own adaptation of the classic Soupe au Pistou. French in origin, it addresses itself to the late spring and summer when fresh basil is at its best.

2/3 **cup dried white navy beans**
2 **medium-size leeks**
3 **tablespoons olive oil**
1 **cup diced carrots, scrubbed but not peeled**
1 **cup peeled and diced celery root***
10 **cups Chicken Stock, or combination beef and chicken**
3/4 **cup Tomato Sauce***
1 **tablespoon salt**
Freshly ground black pepper (20 turns of the mill)

1/4 **teaspoon saffron**
2 **cups string beans, stem end removed, then cut into 2-inch lengths**
2 **cups diced unpeeled zucchini**

SEASONING MIXTURE
3 **cloves garlic, minced**
1/4 **cup chopped parsley**
1/4 **cup Pesto Base***
1/2 **cup freshly grated Parmesan cheese**
1/4 **cup olive oil**

Serves 12

1. Place the dried beans in a bowl and completely cover them with cold or room-temperature water. Let them soak overnight. Rinse and drain the beans. Place them in a saucepan and cover with cold water by 1 inch. Bring the beans to a moderate boil. Turn the heat to low and simmer until tender, about 1 hour. Set aside.

2. Remove the root end of the leeks, then split the leeks in half lengthwise all the way through. Place them under forcefully running warm water to remove all traces of sand. Then cut the white and also the tender light green parts into 1/2-inch pieces (reserve the dark green part for basic Tomato Sauce or stock). The yield should be 2 cups diced leeks.

3. In a large kettle heat the 3 tablespoons olive oil until it is hot but not smoking. Add the carrots, leeks, and celery root; sauté over low heat until soft but not brown.

Add the stock and bring to a simmer over high heat. *Do not cover at any time while the soup is simmering.* Add the tomato sauce and simmer 15 minutes over low heat. Add the salt, pepper, and saffron; simmer a few more minutes.

Add the white beans and the liquid in which they were cooked and simmer a few minutes. Add the string beans and simmer 5 minutes. Add the zucchini and simmer 3 minutes.

4. Place all the ingredients for the seasoning mixture in a bowl. Com-

bine thoroughly, then place in a large soup tureen. Add 1 cup of the simmering soup, beating well. Pour in the remaining soup and serve immediately.

PLAN AHEAD

The soup can be made a day in advance, but the seasoning mixture should be made no more than an hour before serving.

*NOTE

For the celery root, you can substitute an equal amount of celery.

If you haven't made up a batch of Tomato Sauce and stored it in the freezer, you can use the commercially made brand of your choice.

Preferably use fresh Pesto Base rather than frozen.

Avgolemono

In Greek, *avgo* means egg and *lemono* means lemon. Avgolemono is a traditional Greek soup, but because of its simplicity it goes well with many cuisines.

4 cups Chicken Stock	**Salt to taste**
1/3 cup raw rice, rinsed and drained	**1 tablespoon chopped fresh dill**
1 medium-size carrot, cut in circles, scrubbed but not peeled	**2 tablespoons lemon juice**
	1 egg at room temperature

Serves 6

1. In a medium-size saucepan, add the chicken stock. Turn the heat to high. When the stock comes to a simmer, add the rice, carrots, and salt. Cover. Turn the heat to low and simmer 15 minutes. Uncover. Add the dill and the lemon juice to the soup.

2. In a small bowl, beat the egg. Add a little of the simmering soup to the egg in a thin stream, beating all the while. Add about 1 cup of the soup to the beaten egg. This is to warm the egg so it will not curdle when it is added to the soup. Add the egg-soup mixture slowly to the simmering soup, at the same time stirring vigorously with a wire whisk. This will thicken the soup slightly. Serve piping hot.

PLAN AHEAD

This soup is also delicious cold, in which case you should make it a day in advance.

Uncle Vanya's Matchstick Soup

Uncle Vanya was a dreamer. He would have told you to cut them as thin as matchsticks. The vegetables, that is. Idealism is as essential to the Russian soul as beet soup is to the Russian cuisine. To make it authentic, practice your slicing.

4 cups canned Italian tomatoes (measured with their juice)*

10 cups Beef Stock

6 medium beets, washed, peeled, and sliced into thin strips (4 cups)

4 cups sliced onions

1 cup sliced (thin strips) carrots, scrubbed but not peeled

2 cups sliced (thin strips) celery root, peeled*

6 cups shredded white cabbage

Salt to taste

Freshly ground black pepper (20 turns of the mill)

1/4 cup apple cider vinegar

2 tablespoons sugar

4 cups boiled beef, cubed*

1/4 cup chopped parsley

GARNISH

Sour cream

Fresh minced dill

Serves 8–10

1. Pass the tomatoes through a food mill into a bowl. Reserve the puréed tomatoes with their juice; discard the seeds.

2. In a large cooking vessel, heat the beef stock until it reaches a simmer. Add the puréed tomatoes, beets, onions, carrots, and celery root. Cover loosely and allow the soup to simmer for about 1 hour.

Add the cabbage, salt, pepper, vinegar, and sugar. Simmer approximately 20 minutes.

Add the beef cubes and the parsley; simmer another 5 minutes.

Serve piping hot. Each diner individually adds a dollop of sour cream and a sprinkle of minced dill.

PLAN AHEAD

This soup is excellent when made the same day or rewarmed several days later.

*NOTE

Four cups canned Italian tomatoes are contained in one 35-ounce tin.

For the celery root, an equal amount of celery can be substituted.

Use meat from Beef Stock, either brisket or chicken steak.

Mulling Spice Cabbage Soup

1 heaping tablespoon of
   mulling spices*
1 tablespoon butter
1 cup chopped onions
1 medium-size Delicious apple,
   peeled and diced
4 cups shredded red cabbage
3 cups Chicken Stock
1 tablespoon apple cider
   vinegar
1/2 teaspoon sugar

1/2 teaspoon salt
Freshly ground black pepper
   (20 turns of the mill)
1 1/2 cups canned Italian
   tomatoes (measured with
   their juice)
2 tablespoons chopped parsley

GARNISH
Sour cream

Serves 4–6

1. Wrap the mulling spices in cheesecloth.
2. In a 3 to 4-quart enamel saucepan, heat the butter until it foams. Add the onions and sauté over medium heat for about 3 minutes or until they are translucent. Add the diced apple and stir briefly. Add the cabbage. Cook about 1 minute. Add the chicken stock, vinegar, sugar, salt, and pepper. Bring to a simmer.

Add the mulling spices and the tomatoes. (When adding the tomatoes, break each one up by squeezing it in your hand over the saucepan.) Bring to a simmer and cover. Simmer for about 1 hour.

3. Stir in the parsley. Serve piping hot, placing a dollop of sour cream in each bowl.

PLAN AHEAD

This soup stores well in the refrigerator for 3 days. If it is too thick, thin it with more chicken stock.

*NOTE

If you want to mix your own mulling spices rather than purchase it, combine dried orange peel, cloves, cinnamon, nutmeg, and allspice.

Soup, Salad and Pasta Innovations
Curried Cream of Leek and Potato Soup

2 medium-size leeks	1 medium-size Idaho potato,
2 tablespoons butter	peeled and sliced thin
1 tablespoon curry powder	3 cups Chicken Stock
1/4 cup chopped parsley	1/4 cup crème fraîche*
Salt to taste	
Freshly ground black pepper	
(10 turns of the mill)	

Serves 4

1. Remove the root end of the leeks, then split the leeks in half length-wise all the way through. Place them under forcefully running warm water to remove all traces of sand. Then cut the white and also the tender light green parts into 1/2-inch pieces (reserve the dark green part for basic Tomato Sauce or stock). The yield should be 2 cups diced leeks.

2. In a medium-size saucepan, melt the butter until it foams. Add the leeks, and sauté over medium-low heat for about 2 minutes. Turn the heat to the lowest possible setting. Cover the saucepan and simmer another 10 minutes, taking care that the leeks do not burn. Shake the pan occasionally. The leeks should turn quite brown and be almost caramelized.

3. Remove the cover and add the curry powder. Continue to stir for another minute. Then add the parsley, salt, pepper, and potato slices. Sauté about 2 minutes, adding another tablespoon of butter if the mixture is too dry.

4. Pour in the stock and bring the soup to a simmer over high heat. Then turn the heat to low. Cover and simmer the soup approximately 30 minutes or until the potatoes are soft.

Add the crème fraîche and stir well to blend.

5. Pass the soup through a food mill. Alternatively, you can drain the soup, reserving the liquid and placing the solids in the container of a food processor, blend until smooth, and then add the solids to the reserved liquid part of the soup. Heat and serve.

PLAN AHEAD

This soup can be made several days in advance. It also freezes well.

*NOTE

For the crème fraîche you can substitute an equal amount of sour cream or heavy cream.

Sea Nymph Soup

Sea Nymph Soup features watercress, which is from a plant family that includes cabbages, mustards, and cresses. Watercress is so named because it is a cress that loves the water.

1/2 **pound new potatoes**
1 **medium-size leek**
2 **tablespoons butter**
1 **tablespoon flour**
2 1/2 **cups Chicken Stock**
2 **bunches watercress with
    stems removed, washed,
    spun dry, and chopped**

1/2 **teaspoon salt**
**Freshly ground black pepper
    (10 turns of the mill)**
1/2 **cup heavy cream**

Serves 3–4

1. Scrub, steam until tender, peel, then slice the new potatoes.
2. Remove the root end of the leeks, then split the leeks in half lengthwise all the way through. Place them under forcefully running warm water to remove all traces of sand. Then cut the white and also the tender light green parts into 1/2-inch pieces (reserve the dark green part for basic Tomato Sauce or stock). The yield should be 3/4 cup diced leeks.
3. In a 2-quart saucepan, melt the butter until it foams. Add the leeks and sauté over low heat for about 2 minutes or until they are soft. Add the flour, stirring constantly, for about 2 minutes. Add the chicken stock, stirring in a figure-8 motion. Turn the heat to high and bring mixture to a simmer.
4. Add the watercress, salt, pepper, and potatoes. Simmer over low heat for about 5 minutes. Stir in the cream. Turn off the heat and serve.

PLAN AHEAD
Sea Nymph Soup can be made several days in advance and refrigerated. It is also possible to freeze.

Soup, Salad and Pasta Innovations
Cauliflower Court Soup

Cauliflower caught the fancy of Mark Twain who called it a cabbage with a college education. If his Connecticut Yankee had dined at Versailles in the 1700s, he would have found cauliflower graduating *cum laude,* served as a superlative creamed soup fit for princes and paupers and simple farm maidens like Madame Du Barry, who created it for her courtly friend Louis XV.

1 medium-size leek	**Salt to taste**
3 tablespoons butter	**Freshly ground black pepper**
1 pound cauliflower florets	**(10 turns of the mill)**
4 cups Chicken Stock	**1 cup freshly grated sharp**
1 cup milk	**Cheddar cheese, loosely**
2 tablespoons chopped dill	**packed**

Serves 6–8

1. Remove the root end of the leeks, then split the leeks in half lengthwise all the way through. Place them under forcefully running warm water to remove all traces of sand. Then cut the white and also the tender light green parts into 1/8-inch half-rounds (reserve the dark green part for basic Tomato Sauce or stock). The yield should be 1 cup chopped leeks.

2. In a 2-quart saucepan, heat the butter until it foams. Add the leeks; sauté over low heat for about 5 minutes, stirring occasionally. Add the cauliflower florets and the chicken stock. Cover and simmer over low heat 10 minutes or until the cauliflower is tender.

3. Put the soup through the finest blade of a food mill or purée in a blender or food processor.

4. Return the puréed soup to the saucepan. Bring to a simmer. Add the milk, stirring in a figure-8 motion. Add the dill, salt, and pepper. Add the cheese, mixing well until combined. Bring to a simmer and serve immediately.

PLAN AHEAD

This soup can be prepared several days in advance.

French Carrot and Dill Soup

2 tablespoons butter
1 cup chopped onions
3 cups carrots, scrubbed but
    not peeled
1 teaspoon sugar
1 tablespoon chopped parsley

Salt to taste
Freshly ground black pepper
    (10 turns of the mill)
3 cups Chicken Stock
1/4 cup crème fraîche*
1 tablespoon minced fresh dill

Serves 3–4

1. In a 2-quart saucepan heat the butter until it foams. Add the onions; sauté over medium heat for about 3 minutes or until they are translucent. Do not allow to brown.

2. Turn the heat to low and add the carrots, stirring briefly. Add the sugar, parsley, salt, and pepper; stir a few seconds. Add the chicken stock. Turn the heat to high and bring to a simmer. Turn the heat to low. Cover the saucepan and simmer the soup for 15 minutes.

3. Turn off the heat. Strain the soup and reserve the liquid. Place the contents of the strainer (cooked vegetables) into a food processor and purée. Return the puréed vegetable mixture, along with the reserved liquid, to the saucepan.

4. Add the crème fraîche and the dill. Bring the soup to a simmer over low heat, stirring occasionally. Serve piping hot.

PLAN AHEAD

French Carrot and Dill Soup will last several days in the refrigerator and freezes beautifully.

*NOTE

For the crème fraîche, you can substitute an equal amount of sour cream.

Chicken and Watercress Soup with Ham and Shrimp Dumplings

If someone said to me, "Make a Chinese soup, any one you want," this is the one I would choose. When you want a light supper, think about making it. Without trying to be, it's actually dietetic as well as satisfying. You can even make a whole meal of it.

1/3 **cup Chinese mushrooms**
2 **tablespoons mushroom stock (see step 1)**
6 **cups Chicken Stock**

DUMPLINGS
1/2 **pound raw shrimp, weighed with the shell**
1/4 **cup minced Westphalian ham***
1 **scallion, white and green parts included, cut into** 1/8-**inch rounds**
1 **teaspoon sugar**

2 **teaspoons dark soy sauce**
1 **egg**
2 **level tablespoons cornstarch**

1/2 **boneless, skinless chicken breast**
1 **egg white, slightly beaten**
2 **bunches watercress**
6 **fresh water chestnuts***
Freshly ground white pepper (10 turns of the mill)
Salt to taste
1 **teaspoon Oriental sesame oil**

Serves 4–6

1. Rinse the mushrooms and cover with cold water. Soak for 2 hours or until soft. Squeeze the mushrooms over the bowl. Remove the stems. Return the stems to the water in which the mushrooms were soaking and reduce over a low heat until 2 tablespoons remain. Strain the stock, discarding the mushroom stems. Add the mushroom stock to the chicken stock. Quarter the mushrooms.

2. *To make the dumplings:* Shell, wash, drain, dry, and chop the shrimp finely. Place the shrimp in a bowl and add the ham, scallions, sugar, and soy sauce. In a separate bowl, beat together the egg and cornstarch. Then add the egg mixture to the shrimp mixture, stirring with chopsticks until well blended. Place the dumpling mixture in the refrigerator for at least 1 hour.

3. Place the chicken breast in the freezer. When partially frozen, slice in paper-thin pieces, approximately 1 × 1 × 1/8-inch. Mix the chicken slices with the beaten egg white and refrigerate.

4. Cut and discard at least 3 inches of stem off the watercress, then wash and spin-dry.

5. Peel the water chestnuts, then slice in half once, maintaining the round shape.

6. Bring the chicken stock to a simmer in a 2½ to 3-quart saucepan. Into the simmering chicken stock drop the dumpling mixture, 1 full teaspoon at a time, pushing the mixture off the teaspoon with your finger. Use up about half the dumpling mixture, then let the dumplings simmer until they float. Continue to let them simmer for another minute. Remove the dumplings with a metal strainer and place them in a bowl. Repeat the cooking procedure for the remaining half of the dumpling mixture.

7. Return the chicken stock to a simmer. Add the mushrooms and simmer for 2 minutes. Add the watercress and stir with chopsticks. When the soup returns to a simmer, add the chicken pieces and mix well with a figure-8 motion to prevent the chicken pieces from sticking together. When the stock begins to simmer again, add the water chestnuts, cooked dumplings, and pepper. Taste and add salt if necessary. Add the sesame oil. Turn off the heat. Serve immediately.

PLAN AHEAD

The dumplings can be made a day in advance and refrigerated in a covered bowl. All the other preparations can be done early in the day. The actual cooking of the entire soup must be done at the last minute.

*NOTE

For the Westphalian ham, you can substitute prosciutto or any interesting smoked ham.

Fresh water chestnuts are very hard to find outside of an area where there is a Chinese community. This soup works very well by substituting icicle radish, which is a Chinese turnip, also known as daikon. Another substitution would be jícama, which is a Mexican radish.

Clam and Icicle Radish Soup

This is a very light, delicate, and beautiful Fukienese soup. Fukien, a province in China, is near the island of Taiwan and right above Canton and Hong Kong. It is known for its highly refined soups. A Fukien dinner will often include between its eight courses at least four outstanding soups. Although Clam and Icicle Radish Soup is Chinese, it would be appropriate to serve it as a first course preceding any type of meal.

18 littleneck clams, as small as possible
2 tablespoons corn meal
3 cups icicle radish*
5 cups combined Chicken Stock and clam stock (see steps 2 and 4)
1 tablespoon finely shredded ginger

1 tablespoon medium-dry sherry
2 scallions, white and green parts, cut in 1/8-inch rounds
1 teaspoon Oriental sesame oil
2 tablespoons minced smoked ham*

Serves 4–6

1. Scrub each clam thoroughly with a vegetable brush under cold running water. Place the clams in a large bowl with cold water to which the corn meal has been added. Allow them to soak for 1 hour. Remove the clams from the bowl and wash again.

2. *To steam the clams:* The clams must be steamed in a dish with a lip so that the juices that are released while the clams are steaming (the clam stock) are not lost. Use whatever steaming setup you like. I prefer an old-fashioned enamel turkey roaster with a dome-shaped cover. This roasting pan can be easily transformed into a steamer by removing the bottom and top of a tin can. This will create a cylinder. Place the cylinder, which is approximately 3 inches high and 4 inches in diameter, in the bottom of the roasting pan. Fill the pan with water to a depth of 3 inches. Then place the dish in which you have put the clams on top of the cylinder. Cover the top part of the roasting pan with the dome-shaped cover. Turn the heat to high and then steam until the clams open. After about 3 to 5 minutes, start checking the clams. They will not all open at once.

3. While the clams are steaming, peel the icicle radish, rinse, then cut into shreds about 3 inches in length.

4. Lift the clams out of the steamer after they open and place them in a paella dish or an oval-shaped serving dish with a 2-inch lip. When all the clams have opened, line a sieve with two layers of cheesecloth that has been washed and wrung out. Place the sieve over a large Pyrex measuring

cup. Pour the clam stock through the sieve and then into a saucepan, adding enough chicken stock to make 5 cups.

5. Bring the combined chicken and clam stock to a simmer. Add the icicle radish and ginger; simmer, stirring occasionally, for about 3 minutes. Add the sherry and simmer a few seconds. Add the scallions and simmer 30 seconds. Turn off the heat and add the sesame oil. Pour the simmering soup over the clams in the paella dish. Sprinkle with minced ham and serve immediately.

*NOTE

Icicle radish, also called daikon, is a Chinese turnip. Because only 3 cups are required, buy a small one.

For the minced ham, I recommend using Westphalian, prosciutto, or some other interesting smoked ham, such as Harrington smoked ham from Vermont.

Soup, Salad and Pasta Innovations
Pekingese Hot and Sour Soup

This dish is for those who have a well-stocked Chinese pantry. It is my own adaptation of a popular classic Northern Chinese soup. In China Pekingese Hot and Sour Soup differs from this version in three ways. The Chinese use a base of water, whereas I am using chicken stock. They feel the soup has enough ingredients to make it tasty without using a stock, and also, chicken stock is not always easy to come by. Secondly, the Chinese use one vinegar to make the soup sour, perhaps white distilled vinegar or the Chinese red vinegar, whereas I prefer to use four different vinegars, which give the soup more dimensions of flavor. And lastly, they thicken the soup traditionally with chicken blood, whereas I prefer a binder composed of cornstarch dissolved in mushroom stock. Chinese mushroom stock is my own innovation. I like to call it *glace de champignon.* In the recipe, I use water to reconstitute not only the mushrooms but also the tiger lily buds and the tree ears. Although the mushroom water is used for human consumption, tiger lily water and tree ear water are not. But please don't throw them out, as they have a salutary effect on plants. They make sick plants healthy and healthy plants healthier.

1/4 pound boneless raw pork (Boston butt or loin or 1 loin pork chop)
1/4 cup Chinese mushrooms
1/4 cup mushroom stock (see step 2)
12 tiger lily buds*
1 tablespoon dried tree ears*
1 cake fresh bean curd (tofu)
1/4 cup bamboo shoots
1/2 teaspoon sugar
11/2 tablespoons dark soy sauce
1 tablespoon black rice vinegar

2 tablespoons red wine vinegar
1 tablespoon Chinese red vinegar
1 teaspoon balsamic vinegar
2 level tablespoons cornstarch
4 cups Chicken Stock
2 scallions, white and green parts, cut in 1/8-inch rounds
1 teaspoon Oriental sesame oil
Freshly ground black pepper (10 turns of the mill)
1/2 teaspoon Chili Oil
1 egg, beaten

Serves 4–6

1. Partially freeze the pork, then cut into julienne strips.
2. Rinse the mushrooms, then cover with cold water and soak for two hours or until soft. Squeeze the mushrooms over the bowl. Remove the stems. Return the stems to the water in which the mushrooms were soaking and reduce over a low heat until 1/4 cup remains. Strain this mushroom

stock, discarding the mushroom stems. Set aside. Shred the mushrooms. Allow to cool.

3. Cover the tiger lily buds in cold water and soak until soft, about 1/2 hour. Squeeze the tiger lilies over the bowl. Put them in a row and cut off the hard ends. Tie each tiger lily in a knot. This is for aesthetic appeal.

4. Cover the tree ears with cold water and allow to soak for about 1/2 hour or until they are soft. Remove the tree ears from the water and rinse well to remove all traces of sand. Pile them on top of each other and shred.

5. Shred the bean curd by first making slices, then piling them on top of each other and shredding.

6. Slice the bamboo shoots thinly, going with the grain (if you look closely, you will see there are grains running through the bamboo shoots, just like grains of meat). Pile the slices on top of each other, then shred thinly.

7. In a small bowl, combine the sugar, soy sauce, and vinegars.

8. In another small bowl, combine the cornstarch and the cooled, reduced, and strained mushroom stock. This is now called the binder.

9. Bring the chicken stock to a simmer in a medium-sized saucepan. Add the pork shreds and stir with chopsticks. Bring to a simmer again.

Add the mushrooms, tree ears, tiger lily buds, and bamboo shoots. Return to a simmer and cook for 3 minutes over a low heat. Add the bean curd, sugar, soy sauce, and vinegars.

10. Restir the binder and add with one hand while stirring gently in a figure-8 motion to reach the center of the saucepan with the other, until the soup thickens, about 1 minute. Add the scallions, sesame oil, pepper, and chili oil. Stir briefly. Turn off the heat.

11. Slowly pour in the egg with one hand while stirring with chopsticks with the other in a slow figure-8 motion. Do not overmix. Serve immediately.

PLAN AHEAD

The entire soup can be prepared ahead through step 9, and then refrigerated.

Pekingese Hot and Sour Soup is best when cooked and eaten right away, but in the event there is some left over, it can be refrigerated and rewarmed the next day. It can even be frozen for up to one month.

*NOTE

Tiger lily buds are the buds of the tiger lily flower. Once purchased, they can be stored indefinitely in a glass jar on the shelf. They are also sometimes called lily buds, diamond needles, or golden needles.

Tree ears, also called cloud ears, wood ears, or black fungus, actually grow on trees. They are said to have a high calcium content and are given credit for being a blood anticoagulant, hence, a coronary preventative.

Salads

Salad Days

Do you remember your salad days when you were green in judgment and cold in blood and could eat iceberg lettuce with bottled dressing? I prefer thinking of Steamed Shrimp with Rémoulade Sauce. It's delicious, an excellent choice for company as it's easy to serve, you can make it in advance, and most everyone loves shrimp. Or imagining Fresh Green Pea and Cheddar Cheese Salad, in which an ordinary vegetable is prepared in an inventive way. Or picturing Celery Root with Creamy Mustard Dressing, in which an exotic vegetable is demystified. These salads rival anything on an hors d'oeuvre table.

This chapter will take you far away from the salad composed of raw leafy lettuce or a cooked vegetable on raw leafy lettuce. Instead the principal ingredient might be pasta or rice or meat or seafood or chicken or cheese. The difficult part will be which one to make and when to serve it—before a main course, after a main course, or as a main course. For instance, do you want Roasted Pepper and Mozzarella di Bufala Salad for lunch today or before an Italian meal tonight? Perhaps you prefer as a first course a light salad such as Smoked Salmon and Endive with Walnut Vinaigrette, which has just a hint of protein. If you want a salad to take the place of lunch or dinner, Scallop and Caviar Salad would make an outstanding choice. This creative dish of salmon caviar and steamed scallops appeals to all the senses, and goes far beyond most people's expectations of a salad.

If you want a main course salad featuring chicken, you can choose Oriental Chicken Salad, Chicken and Garlic Salad, or Charred Sesame Chicken Salad. You can have a main course pasta salad, as in Tortellini Vegetable Salad with Ham. You can have savory, tart, sweet, lavish, or light salads.

If the salad is not the main course, there is the before-or-after-the-meal issue. In the 1700s a French hygienist recommended eating salads at the end of a meal. He said it "moistens, refreshes, frees the stomach, encourages sleep . . . and tempers the ardors of Venus . . ." Americans of course would reply, What's the point of tampering with Venus? and continue to eat their salads before the main dish as an appetizer course. Traditionally, Europeans prefer salad as the last course so the vinegar in the dressing does not interfere with the wine which accompanies the meal.

Four Persons Wanted

According to the Spanish proverb, four persons are needed to make a good salad: "a spendthrift for oil, a miser for vinegar, a counselor for salt, and a madman to stir it all up."

I agree emphatically. For a good salad, you need a good dressing, and if the dressing is not based on cream, mayonnaise, or cheese, it's probably based on oil and vinegar. I use the spendthrift/miser proportion myself: 3 parts oil to 1 part vinegar. For a simple French dressing, I usually dissolve the salt in the vinegar as the first step, then add a crushed garlic clove. Then I mix in some mustard and then the oil. The fresh pepper last.

As for what particular oils, I like to use olive oil, one that is somewhat lighter than the purest dark green virgin olive oil from the first pressing. Or sometimes I use a combination of olive oil and corn oil, which further lightens a dressing. For an Oriental salad, I often use sesame oil and/or peanut oil. If I want it spicy, I add homemade chili oil. Occasionally I use a fragrant nut oil, such as walnut oil.

On the subject of vinegar, I would recommend hunting around for a good-quality red wine vinegar, the color of which should be nice and deep and not artificial-looking. It must not have over 6 or 7 percent acidity. French red wine vinegars are usually the best. Purchase one in a glass bottle, as a plastic bottle imparts an adverse flavor to the vinegar. Keep in mind that it should taste good on its own.

I often add a little balsamic vinegar to my dressings. It is an aged, unfermented white grape vinegar that comes from Italy. Being very concentrated, balsamic vinegar is too sweet, too intense to use alone. Because of the wonderful bouquet and flavor of both balsamic and red wine vinegar, I would suggest refrigerating them if you don't use them up quickly, say within a month.

When I want a more substantial dressing, I use cream or mayonnaise, in which case I frequently add lemon juice rather than vinegar. This type of dressing forms a natural liaison with crustaceans and also certain vegetables including strong ones like celery root and mild, sturdy ones like cucumbers and romaine.

Besides the oils, vinegars, cream, and mayonnaise, it is good to stock your larder with Dijon and Pommery mustards, anchovy paste, sugar, salt, peppercorns, lemons, Worcestershire sauce, horseradish, chili sauce, sun-dried tomatoes, and olive paste, which is a condiment composed of crushed black or green olives. I find that a few diced sun-dried tomatoes, or a teaspoon of olive paste mixed into the dressing gives it a nice spike.

As for the greens and other fresh ingredients, only the absolute freshest will do. With baking, every mistake shows; with a salad, every ingredient's inadequacy is magnified. You can't cover up poor-quality produce with a magnificent salad dressing.

Selecting the best is an acquired skill that comes from years of shopping and some trial and error. Look for freshness not only at the tops of cauliflower and asparagus but also at the bottoms. See that the asparagus tips are tightly closed. Broccoli should be dark green and snow peas should be bright green with small, underdeveloped peas. Make sure that greens are intensely green with no trace of brown or yellow, whether they be romaine, Bibb, Boston, arugula (an Italian green), or watercress. Seize the opportunity to buy fresh herbs, as there is no substitute for fresh dill, chives, and parsley, all of which should be dark green and aromatic. Ask when the vegetables were delivered. Unless you're at a farmers' market, never shop on Saturday or Sunday or on a Monday morning. Pay attention to the seasons, buying celery root in the fall, asparagus in the spring.

Salad Equipment

I like to serve salads either in wooden salad bowls or on a white oval serving platter. I like white because the colors in the salad don't compete with the serving dish.

To keep lettuce crisp and fresh for two days, I wash it, spin it dry, and then refrigerate it in a cloth bag. For this you will need a plastic salad spin-dry and some cotton bags or tea towels.

Dressings are best made and eaten the same day; however, they will last a few days in the refrigerator if you omit the garlic. For storing dressings, you will need some glass jars.

For tossing, you'll need tossers; for grinding fresh peppercorns, a good pepper mill that will grind coarse and fine; and for chopping, a wooden chopping block.

Soup, Salad and Pasta Innovations
Roasted Pepper and Mozzarella di Bufala Salad

This is a wonderful salad for a light lunch or as an appetizer. The star ingredient is mozzarella cheese made with buffalo's milk instead of cow's milk, which in the past was considered the only authentic mozzarella. Now, because the cow's milk adaptation is becoming increasingly common as the result of a shortage of buffalo milk, mozzarella di bufala is savored. It is not used so much for cooking as simply for eating. Imported from Southern Italy, this fresh milk cheese is available in some specialty cheese stores. Before purchasing, you should ask when it was delivered and taste it to make sure it is not sour.

When I was in Northern Italy recently, I tasted some mozzarella di bufala and it was fresher and better than any I have had in the States, as it does not improve with travel or age. However, the mozzarella di bufala that is sold here is still a treat—amazingly sweet and creamy, tart and chewy at the same time. I encourage you to try it if you haven't already.

If necessary you can substitute cow's-milk mozzarella, but the taste and texture will be different. Buy it from a store that makes it daily, kept in its own whey. For salads, use it the same day, as refrigeration makes cow's-milk mozzarella rubbery. Any remaining portion can be used for cooking.

1 bunch leafy lettuce

6 medium to large fresh peppers, combination yellow Holland, red sweet, and green bell*
1/4 cup chopped parsley
1 teaspoon minced garlic
2 tablespoons olive oil
1/2 teaspoon salt
Freshly ground black pepper (5 turns of the mill)

DRESSING
1 1/2 tablespoons red wine vinegar

1/2 tablespoon balsamic vinegar
1/4 teaspoon salt
1/4 teaspoon Worcestershire sauce
Freshly ground black pepper (15 turns of the mill)
1 teaspoon Dijon mustard
1/4 cup chopped fresh basil *or* 1 tablespoon Pesto Base*
6 tablespoons olive oil

1 pound mozzarella di bufala*

Serves 6–8

1. Wash and spin-dry the lettuce. Wrap in a towel and refrigerate.

2. *To roast the peppers: Method 1,* for on top of a gas range: Place the whole peppers directly on the heating element of the stove. Turn the heat to low. Roast the peppers, occasionally turning with tongs as the skins begin to char. Keep turning until the entire pepper has charred—the more charred, the easier it will be to peel. Using the lowest possible heat, this will take about 20 to 30 minutes. The yellow peppers will char much more quickly than the red.

Method 2, for the broiling unit, whether gas or electric: Preheat the oven to broil. Place the peppers on a rack resting on a shallow roasting pan or a cookie sheet which has been lined with aluminum foil. Broil the peppers 3 inches from the heat source, turning occasionally. Char all sides of the peppers. This will take from 10 to 20 minutes. The yellow peppers will char much more quickly than the red.

3. Place the charred peppers in a brown paper bag for 10 minutes. Remove the peppers from the paper bag. Quarter them, then core and seed. Using a knife, scrape off the charred skins. Cut the peppers into strips about 3/4-inch wide.

Mix the peppers with the parsley, garlic, 2 tablespoons olive oil, 1/2 teaspoon salt, and pepper (5 turns of the mill).

4. Place the vinegars in a bowl. Add the 1/4 teaspoon salt and stir until dissolved. Add the remaining dressing ingredients and mix until well combined.

5. Cut the mozzarella in 1/4-inch slices.

Arrange 8 to 10 individual salad plates with first a lettuce leaf, then a few marinated roasted peppers, a few slices of mozzarella, and a tablespoon or so of dressing. Once the salad has been dressed, serve immediately.

PLAN AHEAD

The marinated roasted peppers will keep for 1 week in the refrigerator in a bowl covered with plastic wrap.

*NOTE

Fresh tomatoes, when available locally, make an excellent substitute for the fresh peppers. Do not roast the tomatoes.

Preferably use fresh Pesto Base rather than frozen.

The best method of storing mozzarella di bufala is to place it in a glass jar and cover it with its whey. When purchasing, ask for extra whey. Refrigerated, it will last several days.

Antipasto Salad

Move this recipe to the top of your "must do" list. It's a crowd pleaser.

1/2 **cup dried chick-peas***
6 ounces smoked sausage such as caccitorini*
1 cup diced comté cheese (or any imported Swiss cheese)
1/2 **cup Niçoise olives**
2 tablespoons chopped parsley
1/2 **cup diced red sweet pepper**
1/2 **cup diced yellow Holland pepper**
1/2 **cup scallions, white and green parts included, cut in** 1/8**-inch rounds**

2 tablespoons olive oil
1 tablespoon red wine vinegar
2 teaspoons balsamic vinegar
Freshly ground black pepper (20 turns of the mill)
3/4 **teaspoon anise seed**

Bibb lettuce leaves

Serves 6–8

1. Place the chick-peas in a bowl and cover with cold water. Cover the bowl and let them soak for 10 hours.

2. Drain the chick-peas. Place them in a small saucepan with a tight-fitting cover. Add 1 cup water. Bring to a boil over high heat, then turn the heat to low. Stir briefly, then cover and simmer over low heat until the chick-peas are tender and all the water has evaporated, approximately 1 to 1 1/4 hours. Remove the chick-peas from the saucepan and allow to cool. You should have about 1 full cup.

3. Remove the casing from the sausage, then slice thin.

4. Combine all the ingredients in a bowl and toss well. Allow the salad to sit at least 1 hour. Arrange the Bibb lettuce leaves around the sides of a platter. Place the antipasto on the lettuce. Serve at room temperature.

PLAN AHEAD

Antipasto Salad is best when made the same day several hours in advance; however, it can be stored in the refrigerator and will last for 1 or 2 days.

*NOTE

I prefer cooking chick-peas from the dried state; however, a time-saving device would be to buy the canned variety, in which case, they should be drained.

For the smoked sausage, you can substitute salami.

Salami and
Summer Squash Salad

This delicious and colorful salad makes a perfect start to an Italian meal.

1 cup finely shredded
    unpeeled yellow summer
    squash
1 cup finely shredded
    unpeeled zucchini
1/2 cup finely shredded carrots
1/2 cup finely shredded red
    sweet pepper
3/4 cup thickly shredded
    provolone
1/2 cup shredded salami
    (soprasata)

1 teaspoon Dijon mustard
Freshly ground black pepper
    (8 turns of the mill)
1 clove garlic, crushed
1 tablespoon chopped parsley
4 tablespoons olive oil
1/4 teaspoon sugar

Curly lettuce leaves

DRESSING
1/2 teaspoon salt
1 tablespoon champagne
    vinegar*

Serves 4–6

1. Place all the shredded vegetables, provolone, and salami in a bowl. Toss well.
2. Dissolve the salt in the vinegar in a small bowl. Then add the mustard, pepper, garlic, parsley, olive oil, and sugar. Stir until well combined. Remove the garlic clove.
3. Pour the dressing over the salad ingredients and toss. Serve on curly lettuce leaves.

*NOTE
You can substitute white wine vinegar for the champagne vinegar.

Steamed Shrimp
with Rémoulade Sauce

This salad makes an excellent hors d'oeuvre. The sauce is a variation on classic rémoulade sauce, which is traditionally made with a base of mayonnaise to which pickles, capers, onions, anchovy paste, and herbs have been added. It is an excellent accompaniment to any cold shellfish, such as lobster, crabmeat, or scallops, as well as blanched vegetables.

2 pounds shrimp (21–25 to the pound)

1 cup mayonnaise
1 hard-boiled egg
1 teaspoon anchovy paste (in tube)
1 teaspoon minced garlic
2 teaspoons chopped sour pickles (preferably cornichons)
2 teaspoons chopped capers, rinsed and drained

2 tablespoons chopped parsley
2 tablespoons snipped chives
2 teaspoons minced fresh tarragon *or* 1 teaspoon dried tarragon
Freshly ground black pepper (20 turns of the mill)
3 tablespoons lemon juice
1 tablespoon Dijon mustard

Serves 8–10

1. Steam the shrimp for 1 minute or until the shells turn pink. Remove the shell. Refrigerate the shrimp.
2. Place the mayonnaise in a mixing bowl. Sieve the hard-boiled egg into the mayonnaise. Add the remaining ingredients; mix well.
3. Arrange the shrimp jutting out like spokes of a wheel, layering them on top of each other on a platter. Place the rémoulade in a dish in the center of the platter. Serve chilled as an appetizer.

PLAN AHEAD

The shrimp and the rémoulade sauce can be made a day in advance and refrigerated. The rémoulade sauce, in fact, tastes better if made several hours in advance.

Scallop and Caviar Salad

1½ pounds bay scallops
3 tablespoons medium-dry
  sherry

DRESSING
⅓ cup mayonnaise
⅓ cup crème fraîche*

¼ cup snipped chives
1½ tablespoons lemon juice
Freshly ground white pepper
  (20 turns of the mill)
1½ ounces salmon caviar

Lettuce leaves

Serves 4–8

1. Place the scallops on a collapsible, stainless-steel vegetable steamer. Sprinkle them with the sherry. Place the steamer in a pot and steam for 5 to 7 minutes, depending on the size. The scallops are done when they turn from cream color to white all the way through. Drain the scallops. Place them in a bowl and refrigerate.

2. Place the mayonnaise, crème fraîche, chives, lemon juice, and pepper in a bowl. Stir until well combined. Fold in the salmon caviar, followed by the scallops, and refrigerate several hours before serving.

3. Remove Scallop and Caviar Salad from the refrigerator one half hour before serving.

4. Serve on lettuce leaves.

PLAN AHEAD
Scallop and Caviar Salad is best made the same day, however, it can be stored in the refrigerator overnight.

*NOTE
For the crème fraîche, you can substitute heavy cream.

Soup, Salad and Pasta Innovations
Emilia-Romagna Salad

Emilia-Romagna is a region in Northern Italy that is considered the country's gastronomic capital. Three regional treasures cherished by the people are their balsamic vinegar made only in Modena, their superlative version of prosciutto called simply Parma ham because it is produced only in the mountains of Parma, and Parmigiano-Reggiano, a hand-made Parmesan cheese which for the last seven centuries has been made in a designated area comprising about one third of Emilia-Romagna.

When you buy Parmesan cheese, you must specify Reggiano, otherwise it will not come from Parma and it will not have the same taste or texture. When you buy it ask when the wheel was cut because from that moment on it starts to dry out. The best way to store it is refrigerated, wrapped in two thicknesses of plastic wrap and then in aluminum foil. Make sure the entire piece of cheese is covered and that a sharp edge does not protrude. Every time you use a portion of the cheese, use new plastic wrap on the remaining portion. Stored this way it will keep at least one month. If the cheese starts to dry out, wrap it in moistened cheesecloth for one day only. If the cheese stays wrapped in the damp cloth longer, it may start to mold.

If you are grating the cheese, for instance for a pasta sauce, always do it at the last minute. In Emilia-Romagna Salad the Parmigiano-Reggiano cheese is sliced instead of grated. It is often served this way in Emilia-Romagna because, being freshly cut, it is moist and at its peak.

1/2 **medium-size romaine**
1/2 **medium-size radicchio**
1 **bunch arugula**
2 **medium-size Belgian endive**

CROUTONS
2 **tablespoons butter**
2 **cloves garlic, crushed**
4 **slices Italian white bread**

DRESSING
1/2 **cup olive oil**
2 **tablespoons wine vinegar**
1 1/2 **teaspoons balsamic vinegar**
2 **teaspoons Dijon mustard**

Freshly ground black pepper (10 turns of the mill)
2 **tablespoons chopped parsley**
1/4 **teaspoon Worcestershire sauce**
1/2 **egg yolk**
1/4 **cup diced prosciutto**
2 **tablespoons diced Niçoise olives *or* 1 teaspoon olive paste**
1 **sun-dried tomato, diced**
2 **cloves garlic, crushed**

2 **ounces Parmesan cheese, sliced***

Serves 6–8

1. Wash and spin-dry the salad leaves. You should have 12 cups. Wrap in a towel and refrigerate.

2. *To make the croutons:* Preheat the oven to 350°. Place the butter and the garlic in a small saucepan. Turn the heat to low. When the butter melts, turn off the heat and let the garlic steep in the butter for 10 minutes. While the garlic is steeping, cut the slices of bread into cubes. Add the bread cubes to the saucepan containing the melted butter and toss to coat. Discard the garlic. Place the bread cubes on a cookie sheet and bake for 10 minutes or until they are brown and crusty. Allow the croutons to cool.

3. Combine the ingredients for the dressing except for the garlic. Blend well. Add the crushed garlic to the dressing and allow it to sit 10 minutes or longer.

4. Remove 1/2 inch at the base of the endive. Slice the endive into thin strips. Break the cold, dry arugula, romaine, and radicchio into approximately 1-inch widths. Place in a large bowl. Add the croutons.

5. Remove the garlic from the dressing. Add the dressing to the salad and toss well. Place on a platter and arrange Parmesan cheese slices on top.

PLAN AHEAD

This dressing can be prepared a day in advance, in which case do not add the garlic. Allow to come to room temperature and mix well before serving. Store in the refrigerator. The croutons can be made several hours in advance.

*NOTE

Buy a large piece of Parmigiano-Reggiano cheese and cut off 2 ounces' worth of slices. If you can't get fresh, substitute 1/4 cup grated Parmesan.

Soup, Salad and Pasta Innovations

Papa Ephram's Low Cal Salad

I used to make this salad for my father, who was always trying to diet. The dressing has a base of chicken stock as opposed to oil. I still enjoy making it from time to time, especially after a return trip from Northern Italy when my waistline is trying to recuperate from sampling four to six pastas twice a day.

2 cups spinach leaves
1 cup watercress, measured after stems have been removed
1/2 cup sliced radishes
1/2 cup alfalfa sprouts
4 slices purple onion

DRESSING
3/4 cup Chicken Stock
2 teaspoons cornstarch
1/4 cup fresh lemon juice

Salt to taste
1 1/2 teaspoons sugar
2 tablespoons olive oil
1 teaspoon horseradish
1 1/4 teaspoons Dijon mustard
1/2 teaspoon paprika
1 clove garlic, minced
1/4 teaspoon Worcestershire sauce
1/4 cup American chili sauce

Serves 4
Dressing yields 1 1/4 cups

1. Wash and spin-dry the spinach leaves and watercress. Place the spinach, watercress, radishes, alfalfa sprouts, and purple onion in a salad bowl.

2. Place the chicken stock and the cornstarch in an enamel saucepan. Simmer over a low heat, stirring with a wooden spoon for about 5 minutes or until it has thickened slightly. Allow to cool.

3. Add to the saucepan the lemon juice, salt, sugar, olive oil, horseradish, mustard, paprika, garlic, Worcestershire sauce, and chili sauce. Using a wire whisk, beat until smooth and blended. Refrigerate.

4. Mix the dressing well before serving. Use half the amount of dressing for the salad ingredients listed above. Place the vegetables in a bowl, add the dressing, then toss until well combined. Serve immediately.

PLAN AHEAD

The remaining salad dressing keeps well for 4 days if stored in the refrigerator.

*NOTE

If desired, add one finely chopped hard-boiled egg to the dressing, or add 2 tablespoons minced onion, 2 tablespoons minced cucumber, and 2 tablespoons minced green bell or red sweet pepper. Depending on these optional additions, the salad dressing will have 20–25 calories per tablespoon.

Romaine and Cucumber with Trudina Dressing

My mother was not typical. She was a vaudeville actress known as Trudina. When she went on vacations, she rode elephants. I was weaned on hard-boiled eggs and grapefruit, which were an important part of her diet. Over the years she has finally succumbed to garlic, sour cream, and all the good stuff.

TRUDINA DRESSING*
1 cup mayonnaise
1/2 cup sour cream
1/2 tablespoon white wine
  vinegar
2 tablespoons lemon juice
2 teaspoons anchovy paste
2 teaspoons minced garlic
1/4 cup chopped parsley
1/4 cup snipped fresh chives

1 teaspoon chopped fresh
  tarragon *or* 1/2 teaspoon
  dried tarragon
1/2 teaspoon salt
Freshly ground black pepper
  (20 turns of the mill)

1 head romaine lettuce
2 cups sliced peeled cucumber
  rounds

Serves 6–8
Yield 2 cups dressing

1. Combine the dressing ingredients. Refrigerate 2 hours. Allow to come to room temperature.

2. Place the romaine and cucumber rounds in a bowl, add 1 1/4 cups or more of the dressing, then toss until well combined. Serve immediately.

*NOTE
Refrigerate the extra dressing for another occasion.

Saint André Salad

1 pound Chinese cabbage
  (Napa)
1 pound red cabbage

SAINT ANDRÉ DRESSING*
2 ounces Saint André triple
  cream cheese
2 ounces blue cheese
1/3 cup plain yogurt

1/4 cup mayonnaise
2 tablespoons chopped parsley
1/2 teaspoon Pommery
  mustard
1 tablespoon lemon juice
1 dash Worcestershire sauce
Freshly ground black pepper
  (10 turns of the mill)

Serves 6
Yield 1 1/4 cups dressing

1. Cut the cabbages in half. Rinse briefly under cold running water and drain well. Then shred. Together they should yield 6 cups.

2. Bring the Saint André and blue cheeses to room temperature. Put them in the food processor and blend with the remaining dressing ingredients.

3. Place the cabbage in a bowl. Add the dressing and toss with wooden spoons until well combined. Serve immediately.

*NOTE
Saint André Dressing can be served as a sauce over asparagus.

Smoked Salmon and Endive with Walnut Vinaigrette

This is an enchanted salad with a romantic touch of smoked salmon. It combines the slightly bitter taste of arugula, radicchio, and endive with the sweet hint of balsamic vinegar.

2 medium-size Belgian endive
1 bunch arugula
1 small head radicchio

DRESSING
1/4 teaspoon salt
2 teaspoons red wine vinegar
1/2 teaspoon balsamic vinegar

1 teaspoon Dijon mustard
Freshly ground black pepper
(5 turns of the mill)
3 tablespoons walnut oil

2 ounces smoked salmon, cut
into triangle shapes, 11/2
inches each

Serves 3–4

1. Remove 1/2 inch of the base of the endive. Then slice into thick strips. Wash and spin-dry. Remove the stems from the arugula. Wash and spin-dry. Separate the radicchio leaves. Wash and spin-dry, then cut into thick strips. This should yield 2 cups radicchio. Place the endive, arugula, and radicchio in a dry towel and refrigerate until crisp.

2. Make the dressing by first dissolving the salt in the vinegars in a small bowl. Then add the mustard, pepper, and walnut oil. Stir until well combined.

3. Place the endive, arugula, and radicchio on a flat white serving platter. Toss with the dressing. Arrange the triangle-cut pieces of smoked salmon on top of the salad in a single layer. Serve immediately.

Soup, Salad and Pasta Innovations

Ambassador Salad with Niçoise Olives
and Sun-dried Tomatoes

This salad has become a staple in my diet. French olives, Italian sun-dried tomatoes, and Holland peppers give Ambassador Salad its name. One of the very Italian ingredients in the dressing is balsamic vinegar, which has become a valuable addition to my pantry. It is referred to as one of the jewels of the Emilia-Romagna region of Northern Italy.

According to Florence Fabricant, in an article she wrote for the New York *Times,* "Traditional balsamic vinegar, which is not a wine vinegar, is made from the unfermented juice of fully ripened white grapes . . . The juice pressed from the grapes is boiled for four to five hours to produce a sweet, intense, amber-colored concentrate. This is put into barrels that have been used previously for vinegar making, renewing a continuous cycle as it picks up the yeasts or 'mother' . . . The older the vinegar the richer and more intense the flavor."

Authentic aceto balsamico is made in Modena and a good bottle that is aged over forty years will cost twenty dollars or more. The bottle will contain about one third of a cup. This used to seem too high a price to pay for vinegar until I tasted it at a private home in Castelfranco just outside of Modena. Many Italians in this region make it in their home and include it in their daughter's dowry.

Use a teaspoon in half an avocado, a dash in the skillet or roasting pan for deglazing. Once opened it should be stored in the refrigerator. There it will keep for one year. When purchasing balsamic vinegar in America, make sure the label reads FROM MODENA.

2 bunches arugula
2–3 Belgian endive
1/4 cup Niçoise olives*
2 tablespoons shredded sun-dried tomatoes
2 tablespoons chopped parsley
1/4 cup shredded yellow Holland pepper

1/2 teaspoon balsamic vinegar
1 teaspoon Dijon mustard
1 garlic clove, crushed
1/4 teaspoon Worcestershire sauce
Freshly ground black pepper (5 turns of the mill)
3 tablespoons olive oil

DRESSING
1/2 teaspoon salt
11/2 teaspoons red wine vinegar

Serves 4

1. Remove the stems from the arugula. Wash and spin-dry. Remove 1/2 inch of the base of the endive. Then cut into slivers. Wash and spin-dry. Combine the arugula and endive. This should yield 8 cups.

2. In a bowl, mix together the arugula, endive, olives, sun-dried tomatoes, parsley, and yellow pepper.

3. Make the dressing by first dissolving the salt in the vinegars. Then add the mustard, garlic, Worcestershire, pepper, and olive oil. Stir well until combined. Remove the garlic clove. Place the dressing over the salad ingredients and toss well. Serve immediately.

*NOTE

If Niçoise olives are not available, another good-quality black olive can be substituted.

Beta Vulgaris Salad

A rose is a rose is a rose, but a beet is a *Beta vulgaris* of the goosefoot family. Just ask any horticulturist. The beet's long stalk of leaves with the swollen root at the end looks like the letter *b*. If you've had dealings with sororities or fraternities or Greek tycoons, you know that the second letter of the Greek alphabet is *beta.*

1½ pounds fresh beets, weighed with the stems and leaves attached

DRESSING
½ cup sour cream
2 teaspoons Pommery mustard
2 tablespoons lemon juice
1 teaspoon sugar

¼ cup snipped chives
¼ cup minced dill
Freshly ground black pepper (10 turns of the mill)
1 teaspoon salt

1 head leafy lettuce (Boston or curly)

Serves 4–6

1. Remove all but 3 inches of the beet stems (this will prevent excessive bleeding). Scrub the beets but do not peel. Steam for about 30 minutes or until tender. This is best determined by piercing a beet with a poultry skewer. Drain the beets, cool slightly, then peel.
2. Combine the dressing ingredients in a bowl. Refrigerate the dressing and beets separately until ready to serve.
3. Remove the beets from the refrigerator then slice. Using a rubber spatula or wooden spoon (so as not to bruise the beets), toss with dressing. Place lettuce leaves on a platter, leaving the center of the platter clear. Place the beet salad in the center and serve.

PLAN AHEAD
Both the beets and the dressing can be prepared a day in advance, but it is preferable not to cut the beets or combine them with the dressing more than ½ hour before serving.

Horseradish Beet Salad

Horseradish Beet Salad makes an excellent accompaniment to gefilte fish or boiled beef or roast chicken. It can also be served as a cold soup, in which case all the reserved beet juice should be used.

**2 cans small whole beets (can
  size 14–16 ounces)**
**1 whole 4-ounce bottle white
  horseradish**
**Freshly ground black pepper
  (15 turns of the mill)**

2 tablespoons corn oil
1/4 cup sugar
**1 tablespoon apple cider
  vinegar**

Serves 8–10

1. Drain beets and reserve juice. Slice them thinly in rounds. Place the beets plus 1 1/2 cups of the reserved juice in a large bowl.
2. Add the horseradish, pepper, corn oil, sugar, and cider vinegar. Toss well to mix. Serve slightly chilled.

PLAN AHEAD
  Horseradish Beet Salad lasts 1 week in the refrigerator.

Summer Corn Salad with Broccoli Florets

4 ears of corn
2 cups blanched broccoli
   florets
1/2 cup sliced purple onion
3/4 cup shredded red sweet
   pepper

DRESSING
1 teaspoon salt
1 tablespoon red wine vinegar

1 teaspoon balsamic vinegar
2 teaspoons Dijon mustard
1 teaspoon minced garlic
1/4 teaspoon Worcestershire
   sauce
2 tablespoons chopped parsley
31/2 tablespoons olive oil

Serves 6–8

1. Shuck the corn then steam or boil for 7 to 10 minutes or until you can smell it. Remove the corn from the steamer and allow to cool. Using a knife, shave off the kernels. This should yield approximately 13/4 cups.

2. In a serving bowl, combine the corn with the broccoli, onion, and red sweet pepper. Toss well until all the ingredients are thoroughly mixed together.

3. Make the dressing by dissolving the salt in the vinegars. Add the remaining ingredients. Stir until well combined.

4. Add the dressing to the corn salad. Toss well. Serve immediately or within the hour.

PLAN AHEAD

Summer Corn Salad with Broccoli Florets can be prepared early in the day through step 3 and refrigerated. Bring to room temperature before serving.

Celery Root with Creamy Mustard Dressing

1 pound celery root
1 1/2 teaspoons salt
1 1/2 teaspoons lemon juice

CREAMY MUSTARD DRESSING
2 tablespoons heavy cream*
1 cup mayonnaise

1/4 cup Pommery mustard
3 tablespoons fresh lemon
   juice
Freshly ground black pepper
   (10 turns of the mill)
1/4 teaspoon balsamic vinegar

Serves 6–8

1. Peel then shred the celery root. Toss the celery root in the salt and lemon juice. Allow to stand for 30 minutes.
2. Place the ingredients for the dressing in a bowl. Mix with a wooden spoon until well combined.
3. Rinse the shredded celery root in cold water. Drain and spin-dry. Place the celery root in a bowl. Add the Creamy Mustard Dressing. Fold and toss until well combined. Serve at room temperature.

PLAN AHEAD
The combined Celery Root with Creamy Mustard Dressing can be stored in the refrigerator for up to 3 days.

*NOTE
For the cream, you can substitute crème fraîche.

Blanched Vegetables
with French Mustard Dressing

FRENCH MUSTARD DRESSING
2 teaspoons salt
1/4 cup red wine vinegar
1 tablespoon balsamic vinegar
1 cup olive oil
1 tablespoon plus 1 teaspoon Dijon mustard
Freshly ground black pepper (20 turns of the mill)
1/4 cup chopped parsley

1 teaspoon Worcestershire sauce
2 cloves garlic, crushed

1 head cauliflower
1 pound string beans
1 cup Niçoise olives
1 1/2 cups well-ripened cherry tomatoes
1 cup sliced purple onions

Serves 8–10
Yield 1 1/4 cups dressing

1. Using a whisk, make the dressing by dissolving the salt in the vinegars. Add the remaining ingredients. Blend well. Allow to sit a few hours.

2. Break the cauliflower into florets, discarding the core. Leave the string beans whole, removing only the stem end. Blanch the cauliflower and string beans separately for about 2 minutes. To stop the cooking and allow the vegetables to retain their color, place the cauliflower and string beans in a bowl of ice-cold water for about 1 minute. Drain.

Place the cauliflower, string beans, olives, tomatoes, and onions in a large serving bowl. Remove the garlic cloves from the dressing. Whisk the dressing, then measure 1/2 cup and pour it over the vegetables. Toss to coat. Serve at room temperature.

PLAN AHEAD

If the dressing is kept separate from the vegetables, the entire dish can be prepared several hours in advance or even can be prepared a day in advance and refrigerated. If making the dressing a day in advance, do not add the garlic until a few hours before serving.

*NOTE

This dressing is great over tossed greens, in which case a tablespoon each of minced shallots and olive paste make an excellent addition.

Cucumbers Dijonnaise

4 medium-size cucumbers
1 teaspoon salt

DRESSING
4 tablespoons olive oil
2 tablespoons red wine
  vinegar
1/4 teaspoon paprika

2 tablespoons Dijon mustard
2 tablespoons sour cream
1/4 cup minced fresh dill

GARNISH
2 tablespoons chopped parsley

Serves 8–10

1. Peel the cucumbers, then split them in half and remove the seeds with a spoon. Slice thinly. Sprinkle them with the salt, then toss well with your hands. Place them in a bowl for 1/2 hour. Squeeze the cucumbers dry and place them in a clean bowl.

2. Combine the ingredients for the dressing in a bowl. Add the cucumbers and mix well. Allow to marinate at least 1 hour.

3. Sprinkle with chopped parsley before serving. Serve at room temperature or slightly chilled.

PLAN AHEAD
Cucumbers Dijonnaise can be made several hours in advance. Refrigerate until 1/2 hour before serving.

Anjou Pear and Macadamia Nut Salad

1/2 cup macadamia nuts
1/4 cup crème fraîche*
1/4 cup mayonnaise
2 tablespoons lemon juice
Grated zest from 1 orange
1 pound fresh well-ripened
    Anjou pears, unpeeled,
    cored, and diced*

1/2 cup diced fennel
1/2 cup raisins
2 tablespoons diced dried
    apricots

Chicory leaves

Serves 6

1. Place the nuts in a strainer and shake off any excess salt.
2. In a bowl mix together the crème fraîche, mayonnaise, lemon juice, and orange zest.
3. Add the macadamia nuts, pears, fennel, raisins, and apricots. Mix until well combined. Serve at room temperature on a bed of chicory leaves.

PLAN AHEAD
    This salad can be made several hours in advance, in which case it should be refrigerated.

*NOTE
    For the crème fraîche you can substitute sour cream.
    For the Anjou pears, any fresh, well-ripened pears can be substituted, such as Bartlett, Comice, and Bosc (in the wintertime). Crisp Delicious apples are another substitute, in which case leave them unpeeled.

Pickled Cabbage with Caraway Seeds

1 head of cabbage, weighing 3
　pounds
2 cups water
1/2 cup cider vinegar
1/3 cup sugar
1 tablespoon caraway seeds

1/2 cup crème fraîche*
1/2 cup mayonnaise
1 tablespoon Dijon mustard
Freshly ground white pepper
　(30 turns of the mill)

Serves 8–10

1. Cut the cabbage in half. Discard a few of the outer leaves. Remove the core and discard. Shred finely. The yield should be 12 cups.

2. In a large bowl, mix together 2 cups water, the vinegar, sugar, and caraway seeds. Stir until the sugar dissolves. Place the cabbage in the bowl and toss well to coat. Allow to marinate overnight.

3. Drain the cabbage. In a large bowl, mix together the crème fraîche, mayonnaise, mustard, and white pepper. Add the drained cabbage and toss well until thoroughly combined with the dressing. Serve slightly chilled.

PLAN AHEAD

Pickled Cabbage with Caraway Seeds is best when made the same day but will last a few days in the refrigerator.

*NOTE

For the crème fraîche you can substitute sour cream.

Artichoke and Sweet Pickle Salad

1 can artichoke hearts (14
  ounces) in water

DRESSING
2 tablespoons olive oil
2 tablespoons mayonnaise
2 teaspoons Dijon mustard

1 teaspoon sugar
Freshly ground black pepper
  (10 turns of the mill)
1 teaspoon red wine vinegar
1 teaspoon balsamic vinegar
1/4 cup diced purple onions
1/4 cup diced sweet pickles

Serves 3–4

1. Drain the artichoke hearts, then rinse and drain again. Place them in a bowl of ice water and refrigerate for 1/2 hour.
2. Place the ingredients for the dressing in a bowl. Stir until well combined.
3. Drain the artichoke hearts first in a strainer and then on paper towels. Cut each artichoke heart in quarters, then drain again on paper towels.
  Add the artichoke hearts to the dressing and toss well to coat. Serve slightly chilled.

Fennel and Fresh Mushroom Salad

1/2 pound fresh mushrooms,
  sliced very thin
1 cup diced fennel
1/2 cup Parmesan cheese
  slices, about 1 inch by 1
  inch by 1/8 inch

DRESSING
1 teaspoon salt
1 tablespoon lemon juice
Freshly ground black pepper
  (10 turns of the mill)
3 tablespoons olive oil

Serves 6

1. Place the mushrooms, fennel, and Parmesan cheese in a bowl; mix together.
2. Make the dressing by dissolving the salt in the lemon juice in a small bowl. Add the pepper and olive oil. Stir until well combined.
3. Add the dressing to the bowl containing the mushrooms, fennel, and Parmesan cheese. Toss well. Serve immediately or within 15 minutes, as after that the mushrooms begin to release their juices.

Fresh Green Pea and Cheddar Cheese Salad

2 pounds fresh green peas, unshelled*
1/3 cup heavy cream
1/2 cup finely diced sharp Cheddar cheese

1/2 cup chopped purple onions
Freshly ground black pepper (10 turns of the mill)

Serves 4–6

1. Shell the peas and steam about 3 minutes or until tender. Place in a bowl of ice water for 1 minute. This will stop the cooking and hold the color. Drain the peas in a strainer over a bowl.

2. Put the cream in a large saucepan. Heat until warm over a low heat. Turn the heat off. Add the cheese and stir until it is half melted. Add the onions and stir until combined. Remove from the heat source.

3. Place the peas in a serving bowl. Pour the contents of the saucepan over the peas. Add the pepper. Fold the mixture until well combined. Serve at room temperature.

PLAN AHEAD

Fresh Green Pea and Cheddar Cheese Salad can be made a day in advance.

*NOTE

Frozen peas can be substituted. One 10-ounce package is the equivalent of 2 cups. If using frozen peas, steaming is not necessary; merely defrost in a strainer set over a bowl. This will take approximately 2 hours.

If desired, Fresh Green Pea and Cheddar Cheese Salad can be served on lettuce leaves.

Fresh Broccoli
and Purple Onion Salad

DRESSING
1 clove garlic, crushed
1 teaspoon Dijon mustard
1/2 teaspoon salt
1 teaspoon balsamic vinegar
2 teaspoons red wine vinegar
3 tablespoons olive oil
Freshly ground black pepper
  (10 turns of the mill)

1 medium-size bunch of
  broccoli
3/4 cup diced purple onions
3/4 cup diced roasted peppers
  (from a jar)

Serves 6

1. Crush the garlic and place in a large bowl. Add the mustard, salt, and vinegars. Stir well until the salt has dissolved. Add the olive oil and the pepper. Mix well.

2. Cut the broccoli into 3 cups of florets and sliced stems (peel stem before slicing). Blanch the broccoli. Plunge into ice-cold water, then drain.

3. Remove the garlic clove from the dressing. Place the blanched broccoli, onions, and roasted peppers in the bowl with the dressing. Toss well. Serve immediately or within the hour.

PLAN AHEAD
Dicing the vegetables and preparing the dressing can both be done early in the day. Combining the vegetables with the dressing should not be done more than one hour before serving.

Chick-pea Salad

1/2 pound dried chick-peas
2 cups Chicken Stock
1 cup chopped celery
1/2 cup chopped celery leaves
1/3 cup chopped cilantro
  leaves*
2 scallions, white and green
  parts, cut in 1/8-inch rounds

Salt to taste
Freshly ground black pepper
  (10 turns of the mill)
1 teaspoon balsamic vinegar
2 teaspoons red wine vinegar
3 tablespoons olive oil

Serves 6

1. Place the chick-peas in a bowl and cover with cold water. Cover the bowl and let them soak 10 hours. Drain the chick-peas, then place in a medium-size saucepan with a tight-fitting cover. Add the chicken stock. Bring to a boil over high heat, then turn the heat to low. Stir briefly, then cover and simmer until the chick-peas are almost tender, about 45 minutes to 1 hour. At the end of the cooking period, there should be no stock remaining. Allow to cool.

2. Add the celery, celery leaves, cilantro, scallions, salt, pepper, vinegars, and olive oil to the cooled chick-peas. Toss until well combined. Serve at room temperature.

PLAN AHEAD
Chick-pea Salad can be made a day in advance and refrigerated. Any portion that is left over will be good the following day.

*NOTE
Cilantro is also known as Chinese parsley or fresh coriander.

Calliope Salad
with Avocado Dressing

Because of the cutting of the vegetables into rounds and circles, this salad honors in its title the old-fashioned calliope.

1 medium-size purple onion
1 large, well-ripened beefsteak
tomato
1 medium-size cucumber

DRESSING
1 medium-size well-ripened
avocado
1 cup Chicken Stock
2 tablespoons lime juice

2 tablespoons milk
2 tablespoons heavy cream
1/4 cup sour cream
1 teaspoon salt
Freshly ground white pepper
(10 turns of the mill)
1/2 teaspoon sweet paprika
2 tablespoons chopped
cilantro leaves*
2 tablespoons snipped chives

Serves 4

1. Peel the onion and slice thinly. Each slice should be whole and round.

2. Slice the tomato, maintaining the round shape, in 1/4-inch circles. Peel and slice the cucumbers in 1/4-inch circles.

Arrange the sliced onions, tomatoes, and cucumbers in an overlapping pattern.

3. Cut the avocado in half and scoop out the meat. Place the avocado meat plus all the ingredients for the dressing with the exception of the chives in the container of a food processor, and using the on-and-off method, blend until smooth. Pour the avocado dressing over the onions, tomatoes, and cucumbers. Sprinkle with chives. Serve immediately.

PLAN AHEAD

The dressing can be prepared several hours in advance and refrigerated.

*NOTE

Cilantro is also known as Chinese parsley or fresh coriander.

Gazpacho Salad

Made from the chopped raw vegetables traditionally used in gazpacho soup, Gazpacho Salad is an interesting twist on a cold, spicy classic.

1 medium-large cucumber	**1 tablespoon apple cider**
1 green bell pepper	**vinegar**
1 red sweet pepper	**1 teaspoon Dijon mustard**
1 cup halved cherry tomatoes	**3 tablespoons olive oil**
1/2 cup sliced purple onions	**2 tablespoons chopped parsley**
	1 teaspoon Hot Sauce*
DRESSING	
1 teaspoon salt	**6 leaves Bibb lettuce**

Serves 6

1. Peel the cucumber, then cut in half lengthwise. Scoop out the seeds. Cut each half in half lengthwise, then dice. You should have about 2 cups.

2. Split the peppers in half and remove the seeds and membranes. Then shred. You should have about 3 cups combined green and red peppers.

3. Place the cucumber, peppers, tomatoes, and onions in a bowl and toss.

4. In a small bowl, dissolve the salt in the vinegar. Add the mustard, oil, parsley, and Hot Sauce. Stir until well combined. Pour the dressing over the vegetable mixture and toss well. Serve at room temperature.

PLAN AHEAD

Gazpacho Salad can be made several hours in advance. Leftovers can be eaten the next day, but this is not a salad that improves with age.

*NOTE

For the Hot Sauce you can substitute 1/4 teaspoon Tabasco sauce.

Guacamole Salad

DRESSING
1 small tomato
2 scallions, chopped
2 teaspoons olive oil
1 1/2 tablespoons lemon juice
1/2 teaspoon Hot Sauce*
Salt to taste
Freshly ground black pepper
   (5 turns of the mill)
1/2 teaspoon cumin

1 whole well-ripened avocado
Romaine lettuce leaves
1/4 cup diced red sweet pepper
10 black olives

Tortilla chips

Serves 3–4

1. Bring a small saucepan of water to a boil; add the tomato and boil for approximately 10 minutes. Drain and peel. Squeeze the seeds out and discard; chop the tomato. Chill in the freezer for 10 minutes. Place the chopped tomato in a small bowl. Add the scallions and the olive oil. Mix well. Add the lemon juice, Hot Sauce, salt, pepper, and cumin. Stir until the dressing is well blended.

2. Cut the avocado in half then peel. Cut the avocado into 1/2-inch slices, lengthwise; place the slices on a bed of romaine lettuce leaves. Arrange the red pepper and black olives on top. Spoon the dressing over the salad. Serve with tortilla chips.

PLAN AHEAD
You can make the dressing several hours in advance.

*NOTE
For the Hot Sauce you can substitute 1/8 teaspoon Tabasco sauce.

Avocado and Smoked Salmon Salad

DRESSING
1/2 cup crème fraîche*
2 tablespoons milk
1 tablespoon lemon juice
1 teaspoon chopped parsley
1/4 cup snipped chives
Freshly ground white pepper
    (10 turns of the mill)

1 whole well-ripened avocado
1/4 pound thinly sliced smoked
    salmon

1 head leafy or Bibb lettuce
1 tablespoon black sesame
    seeds*

Serves 3–4

1. Combine the ingredients for the dressing in a bowl.
2. Cut the avocado in half then peel. Cut the avocado into 1/8-inch slices, lengthwise.
3. Cut the salmon in approximately 2-inch pieces.
4. Make a bed of lettuce on a platter. Arrange the avocado slices on the lettuce. Place the salmon slices on top of the avocado. Spoon the dressing over the salad. Sprinkle with the black sesame seeds. Serve immediately.

*NOTE

For the crème fraîche, you can substitute 1/4 cup sour cream plus 1/4 cup heavy cream.

Black sesame seeds can be purchased in Japanese or Chinese grocery stores.

Eggplant à la Russe

1 medium eggplant,
  approximately 1 pound
3 tablespoons olive oil
1 cup diced Spanish onions
1 cup diced red sweet pepper
1 teaspoon salt
Freshly ground black pepper
  (10 turns of the mill)
1 teaspoon sugar
1 cup Tomato Sauce*

2 tablespoons chopped parsley
1 teaspoon fresh thyme *or* 1/2
  teaspoon dried thyme
1 teaspoon fresh oregano *or*
  1/2 teaspoon dried oregano
1 tablespoon lemon juice

Lettuce leaves
12–16 black olives

Serves 6–8

1. Preheat the oven to 350°. Prick the eggplant several times with a poultry skewer to avoid its exploding in the oven. Place the eggplant on the middle rack of the oven. Place a shallow roasting pan containing 1 inch of water directly below it on the second oven rack. Bake the eggplant for 1 hour or until it has shriveled. Remove the eggplant from the oven. Peel it, then chop the pulp with 2 heavy knives until it is pasty but still has some chunky consistency. This should yield about 1 1/2 cups.

2. In a 10-inch skillet, heat 2 tablespoons of the olive oil. Add the onions; sauté over medium heat about 2 minutes or until translucent.

Add the red pepper; sauté 2 minutes or until soft.

Add salt, pepper, sugar, tomato sauce, and eggplant. Simmer 1 minute. Turn off the heat.

Add the parsley, thyme, oregano, lemon juice, and the remaining 1 tablespoon of olive oil. Mix well. Allow to come to room temperature.

3. Place individual portions on lettuce leaves, dot with black olives, and serve.

PLAN AHEAD

Eggplant à la Russe can be made in advance and will last up to a week in the refrigerator.

*NOTE

If you haven't made up a batch of Tomato Sauce and stored it in the freezer in small glass jars as recommended, you can use the commercially made brand of your choice.

Greek Eggplant Salad

1 medium eggplant,
   approximately 1 pound
2 scallions, white and green
   parts included, cut in
   1/8-inch circles
1/3 cup mayonnaise
3 tablespoons chopped parsley
2 tablespoons chopped fresh
   dill

1 clove garlic, minced
1 tablespoon red wine vinegar
1/2 teaspoon salt
Freshly ground black pepper
   (15 turns of the mill)

Pita bread

Serves 6–8

1. Preheat the oven to 350°. Prick the eggplant several times with a poultry skewer to avoid its exploding in the oven. Place the eggplant on the middle rack of the oven. Place a shallow roasting pan containing 1 inch of water directly below it on the second oven rack. Bake the eggplant for 1 hour or until it has shriveled. Remove the eggplant from the oven. Peel it, then chop the pulp with 2 heavy knives until it is pasty but still has some chunky consistency.

2. Place the eggplant in a bowl along with the scallions, mayonnaise, parsley, dill, garlic, vinegar, salt, and pepper. Mix well, then refrigerate for 1 day.

3. Serve the Greek Eggplant Salad with heated pita bread.

PLAN AHEAD

Greek Eggplant Salad should be made at least 1 day in advance and lasts for 3 days in the refrigerator. Serve at room temperature.

Eggplant in Garlic Sauce

Eggplant in Garlic Sauce is an Oriental version of ratatouille. It is much better when made a day in advance, or at the very least early in the day for the evening meal. Serve it as a first course, or as a salad to go with roast chicken, leg of lamb, or any other roast, broiled, or barbecued meat, fish, or fowl. It will last a week in the refrigerator, if you hide it in the back. Before the week ends, turn leftover Eggplant in Garlic Sauce into one of my favorite pasta sauces, Salsa Forte.

1/3 **cup Chinese dried mushrooms***

1/4 **cup combined mushroom stock (see step 1) and Chicken Stock**

1 **medium eggplant, 1–1**1/4 **pounds**
1 **teaspoon salt**
1 **medium-size red sweet pepper**
1 **medium-size yellow Holland pepper***
2 **cloves garlic, minced**

2 **scallions, white and green parts included, cut in** 1/4**-inch rounds**

SEASONING SAUCE
2 **teaspoons Hot Sauce***
1 **tablespoon dark soy sauce**
1 **tablespoon red wine vinegar**
1 **teaspoon sugar**
1/3 **cup Tomato Sauce***
2 **tablespoons medium-dry sherry**

3 **tablespoons peanut oil**

Serves 4–6

1. Rinse the mushrooms, cover with cold water, and soak for 2 hours or until soft. Squeeze the mushrooms over the bowl. Cut off the stems and quarter them. Return the stems to the mushroom water. In a small saucepan, reduce the liquid slowly until 1 tablespoon of mushroom stock remains. Strain the stock. Discard the stems. Add enough chicken stock to yield 1/4 cup.

2. Trim off the ends of the eggplant and discard. Cut the eggplant into eighths lengthwise. Cut the slices into 1-inch cubes. Sprinkle with the salt and place on a cookie sheet, with a paper towel and chopping block on top. Let stand 30 minutes or longer. Rinse, drain, and dry the eggplant cubes well.

3. *To triangle-cut the peppers:* Cut the peppers in half from the stem end all the way through. Carefully remove all traces of seed and membrane. Cut the peppers into 3/4-inch slices. Then cut each slice into 3 triangles.

4. Organize a tray with the eggplant, garlic, scallions, peppers, and mushrooms.

5. In a bowl combine the ingredients for the seasoning sauce.

6. Place a wok over high heat for about 1 minute or until it smokes. Add the peanut oil and heat until it is hot but not smoking. Add the eggplant cubes; stir and press lightly to aid the browning. Cook over high heat until fairly soft and slightly scorched, about 3 to 5 minutes. Add the garlic, scallions, peppers, and mushrooms; stir-fry another minute.

7. Restir the seasoning sauce and add it to the wok, continuing to stir-fry another minute. Add the combined mushroom and chicken stock, and continue to stir-fry another minute or two or until the sauce has formed a glaze over the vegetables. Empty the contents of the wok into a dish and allow to cool to room temperature.

PLAN AHEAD

Eggplant in Garlic Sauce improves with age and should be made at least a day in advance. It will last a week in the refrigerator.

*NOTE

Any dried mushroom can be substituted for the Chinese.

For the yellow pepper you can substitute green bell pepper.

For the Hot Sauce, you can substitute ½ teaspoon Tabasco sauce.

If you haven't made up a batch of Tomato Sauce and stored it in the freezer in small glass jars as recommended, you can use the commercially made brand of your choice.

Spicy Pepper Salad

Spicy Pepper Salad plays a crucial role in Chinese Pepper Pasta. No matter how much you like this salad, you must save one cup!

This recipe is an Oriental version of Italian marinated roasted peppers. It differs in the seasoning and the cooking technique. The Chinese scorch their peppers in a wok instead of under or over a direct flame. This technique is only successful if the water has been extracted from the peppers, which is done by salting then weighting them down on paper towels.

Spicy Pepper Salad makes a great appetizer. It is visually appealing because of the attractive triangle cut, and also because of the bright red, green, and yellow peppers. Yellow peppers from Holland are happily available almost all year long now. They are beautiful, and even sweeter than red sweet peppers. The only disadvantage is that they are expensive.

Because Spicy Pepper Salad actually improves with age up to one week, you will have a chance to see which way you enjoy it the most. When you get down to the last cup, if you are not saving it for Chinese Pepper Pasta, you can use it in Salsa Forte as a substitute for the leftover Eggplant in Garlic Sauce.

1 1/2 pounds fresh peppers (combination of red sweet, green bell, and yellow Holland)	**2 teaspoons Hot Sauce***
	2 teaspoons red wine vinegar
	1/2 teaspoon sugar
1 teaspoon salt	**1 1/2 tablespoons peanut oil**

SEASONING SAUCE
1 tablespoon light soy sauce

Serves 4–6

1. *To triangle-cut peppers:* Cut the peppers in half from the stem end all the way through. Carefully remove all traces of seed and membrane. Cut the peppers into 3/4-inch slices. Then cut each slice into 3 triangles. The yield should be 4 cups peppers.

2. Place the peppers on a cookie sheet and sprinkle them with the salt. Cover with paper towels, then add a weight such as a heavy chopping block plus a pot filled with water. Let them stand at least 1 hour. Drain the peppers well.

3. Combine the ingredients for the seasoning sauce.

4. Place a wok over high heat for about 1 minute or until it smokes. Add the peanut oil; heat until hot but not smoking. Add the peppers; stir-fry for

4 to 5 minutes, pressing down on them with a spatula to aid the scorching. If they are charring too fast, turn down the heat.

5. Restir the seasoning sauce and add it to the wok, continuing to stir-fry until all the sauce has absorbed into the peppers. Empty the contents of the wok into a dish and allow to become room temperature.

PLAN AHEAD

This dish improves with age and should be made at least 1 day in advance. Stored in the refrigerator it will last 1 week. This room-temperature salad should never be reheated.

*NOTE

For the Hot Sauce you can substitute ½ teaspoon Tabasco sauce.

Soup, Salad and Pasta Innovations

Sichuan Sweet and Sour Cabbage

Sichuan Province, located in the Western part of China, is a hot, tropical inland region where people grow their own spices and chili peppers. Sometimes they actually eat chili peppers raw—seeds, membranes, and all. It makes them perspire, which cools them off. Their food for the most part is hot and fiery. This mild version of Sichuan Sweet and Sour Cabbage works beautifully with American fare.

2 pounds Chinese cabbage
  (Napa)
1½ tablespoons salt
2 tablespoons peanut oil
2 tablespoons shredded ginger
⅓ cup rice vinegar
3 tablespoons sugar
2 medium scallions, white and
  green parts included, cut
  into ⅛-inch rounds

2 tablespoons chopped
  cilantro leaves*
1 teaspoon Chili Oil*
1 tablespoon Oriental sesame
  oil

Serves 4–6

1. Split the cabbage in two. Remove the core and discard. Shred the cabbage. Place the shredded cabbage on a large plate and toss with salt. Cover with paper towels. Place a heavy, flat weight over the paper towels and let stand for about 2 hours. Squeeze the liquid from the cabbage with your hands.

2. Place a wok or iron skillet over medium heat for about 1 minute. Add the peanut oil and turn the heat to low. Add the ginger and sauté for about 1 minute.

Turn off the heat. Add the vinegar and sugar. Turn the heat to low and stir until the sugar dissolves. Add the scallions and cilantro. Stir 30 seconds.

3. Turn off the heat. Add the chili oil and sesame oil. Pour the sauce over the cabbage and toss well. Serve at room temperature.

PLAN AHEAD

Refrigerated, Sichuan Sweet and Sour Cabbage will last 3 days.

*NOTE

Cilantro is also known as Chinese parsley or fresh coriander.

You can make your own Chili Oil, or you can use the commercially made brand of your choice.

Oriental Bean Sprout Salad with Spicy Sesame Dressing

1/4 cup pine nuts
2 cups mung bean sprouts
1 cup shredded carrots, scrubbed but not peeled
1/2 cup shredded red sweet pepper
2 scallions, white and green parts included, cut into thin 3-inch strips

DRESSING
1 teaspoon minced garlic
1 1/2 tablespoons Oriental sesame oil
1 1/2 tablespoons peanut oil
3 tablespoons light soy sauce
2 teaspoons sugar
3 tablespoons red wine vinegar
1 teaspoon Hot Sauce*

Serves 3–4

1. Preheat the oven to 325°. Roast the pine nuts on a cookie sheet or in an iron skillet for 5 to 10 minutes or until they are golden brown. Remove them from the oven. Allow to cool.

2. Place a wok or iron skillet over high heat for about 2 minutes or until it smokes. Add the bean sprouts. Allow to scorch, shaking the wok occasionally to avoid sticking. This will take 1 1/2 to 2 minutes. Flip and scorch on other side. Remove from the wok and allow to cool.

3. Place the carrots, red pepper, and scallions in a salad bowl. Toss. Add the cooled bean sprouts and pine nuts. Toss.

4. Combine the ingredients for the dressing in a bowl. Add the dressing to the vegetables and pine nuts. Toss well and serve immediately.

PLAN AHEAD
The pine nuts can be roasted early in the day. The bean sprouts can be scorched and cooled several hours in advance. The vegetables can be shredded early in the day and refrigerated, but the salad dressing should not be combined with the vegetables until ready to serve.

*NOTE
For the Hot Sauce you can substitute 1/4 teaspoon Tabasco sauce.

Spicy Stir-fried Vegetable Salad

The Chinese are masters at cooking vegetables. Because of the stir-fry technique, vegetables retain all their vitamins, color, and crunch. Students frequently ask if Chinese food can be rewarmed because of all the last-minute stir-frying. The answer is no, but it can be served at room temperature. The Chinese are infinitely more concerned with texture than temperature. This beautiful array of seasonal vegetables has been served hot at many a party I have catered, but it is also delicious as part of a buffet of room-temperature salad offerings. To have the vegetables at their best, stir-fry them an hour or so before serving. When making this dish, it is best not to have a preconceived notion of what vegetables to use. Instead, choose whatever is fresh and colorful. In the spring, slant-cut asparagus would be a natural substitute for the broccoli. In the early summer I love to use sugar snap peas.

   In China, vegetable dishes are frequently cooked in poultry fat, which gives them an enriched flavor. Save the fat from the bottom of the roasting pan the next time you roast a bird for your family dinner. Place it in a covered glass jar. It stores for months in the refrigerator or one year in the freezer.

1/4 cup Chinese dried
   mushrooms
1 medium-size bunch of
   broccoli
15 small shallots

SEASONING SAUCE
1/2 cup Chicken Stock
1 1/2 tablespoons oyster sauce
2 teaspoons Hot Sauce*
2 teaspoons dark soy sauce

BINDER
2 level teaspoons cornstarch
   dissolved in:
1 tablespoon medium-dry
   sherry

2 tablespoons poultry fat*
1 medium-size seeded and
   triangle-cut red sweet
   pepper
1 medium-size seeded and
   triangle-cut yellow Holland
   pepper
1/4 cup diced smoked ham
1/2 teaspoon sugar
10 fresh water chestnuts,
   peeled and sliced*

Serves 6

   1. Cover the mushrooms with cold water and soak for 2 hours or until soft. Squeeze, cut off the stems, and dice.

2. Cut the broccoli into 3 cups of florets. Blanch the florets. Plunge them into ice-cold water, then drain.

3. Blanch the shallots, then peel. Leave them whole.

4. Combine the ingredients for the seasoning sauce.

5. Mix the binder.

6. Place a wok over high heat for about 1 minute. Add the poultry fat, then turn the heat to low.

Add the shallots and sauté for 2 minutes.

Turn the heat to high. Add the broccoli and mushrooms; stir-fry ½ minute. Add the red peppers, yellow peppers, and the ham; stir-fry 1 more minute. Add the sugar and the seasoning sauce. Bring to a boil. Add the water chestnuts. Mix briefly.

7. Restir the binder. Add it to the wok all at once, stirring rapidly until sauce thickens. Empty the contents of the wok into a large flat platter with a lip. Serve at room temperature.

*NOTE

For the Hot Sauce you can substitute ½ teaspoon Tabasco sauce.

Use any kind of poultry fat—chicken, turkey, duck, or goose. You can also substitute peanut oil.

If you cannot find fresh water chestnuts, omit them. I never use the canned. Just add more of whatever green vegetable you have chosen.

Oriental Spicy Chicken Salad

I originally learned this dish from Madame Grace Zia Chu in 1967. It was my introduction to Chinese cooking.

The Chinese have a whole category of room-temperature dishes. They usually are part of a first course at a banquet. Perhaps ten or more different items will be attractively displayed on a very large banquet platter. This chicken salad is often one of them. A dish like this is also served as part of an Oriental meal. Besides using my adaptation as part of a Western meal, I can't think of a better summer lunch.

1–2 medium-size leeks
2 whole chicken breasts (12–14 ounces each)
4 cups shredded Chinese cabbage (Napa)

DRESSING
2 tablespoons peanut oil
1 teaspoon Sichuan peppercorns (measured after being ground in pepper mill)

1/3 cup scallions, white and green parts included, cut into 1/4-inch rounds
1/2 cup diced red sweet pepper
2 cloves garlic, minced
2 teaspoons minced ginger
1 tablespoon dark soy sauce
1 tablespoon hoisin sauce
2 teaspoons honey
1 teaspoon Hot Sauce*

Serves 4–6

1. Remove the root end of the leeks, then split the leeks in half lengthwise all the way through. Place them under forcefully running warm water to remove all traces of sand. Then cut the green part only into 3-inch pieces (reserve the white part for use in other recipes). The yield should be 2 cups cut leeks.

2. In a 2-quart saucepan with a tight-fitting cover, bring 2 inches of water to a rolling boil. Add the chicken breasts. Place the leeks on top. Cover, turn the heat to low, and simmer 20 minutes or until the chicken breasts are cooked all the way through.

Remove the chicken breasts from the saucepan and allow to drain. Reserve the chicken stock for another use. Remove the skin, then shred the chicken breasts with the fingers. Allow the chicken to cool.

3. Place the chicken and cabbage in a large bowl.

4. Place a wok or iron skillet over high heat for about 1 minute. Add the peanut oil and heat until hot but not smoking. Turn the heat to low. Add the ground Sichuan peppercorns and stir a few seconds.

Add the scallions, red pepper, garlic, and ginger and stir over high heat for about 1 minute. Remove the wok from the heat source. Add the soy sauce, hoisin sauce, honey, and Hot Sauce, stirring well.

5. Pour the dressing into the bowl over the chicken and cabbage. Toss until well combined. Serve immediately.

PLAN AHEAD

Oriental Spicy Chicken Salad is best eaten immediately; however, the preparations can be done early in the day.

*NOTE

For the Hot Sauce you can substitute ¼ teaspoon Tabasco sauce.

Charred Sesame Chicken Salad

If you look at the following two recipes you will see that the marinade in one is almost identical to the dressing in the other. Yet the two recipes taste entirely different. In the Charred Sesame Chicken Salad the chicken breasts are marinated raw for twenty-four hours then run under a fast broiler, which gives them a crusty, charred exterior. The Sesame Chicken Salad is made by poaching chicken breasts, then shredding them by hand and tossing the shreds with Sesame Dressing. It's a spicy change from the mayonnaise-based chicken salad we are used to eating in America.

I love to serve Charred Sesame Chicken Salad as a room-temperature appetizer for my catering assignments and Sesame Chicken Salad for summer lunches as well as large buffets.

**2 pounds boneless skinless
chicken breasts**

MARINADE
3 medium-size garlic cloves
3/4 cup sesame paste*
**1/3 cup steeped black Chinese
tea***
1/4 cup dark soy sauce
1 1/2 tablespoons Chili Oil*
**2 tablespoons Oriental sesame
oil**

2 tablespoons sugar
**2 tablespoons red wine
vinegar**
**1/2 cup scallions, white and
green parts, cut into 1/8-inch
rounds**

GARNISH
Watercress

Serves 4–6

1. Remove all traces of fat and cartilage from the chicken breasts. Each whole chicken breast will yield 2 pieces.
2. Mix together the ingredients for the marinade, ideally in a food processor. If using a food processor, add the garlic cloves first. After they are minced, add the remaining marinade ingredients except for the scallions. Process until smooth. Stir in the scallions (do not process).
3. Place the chicken breasts in a bowl. Add the marinade, making sure all the chicken is well coated. Cover the bowl and place the chicken in the refrigerator for 24 hours.
4. Preheat the oven to broil for at least 20 minutes. Place the marinated chicken on a rack resting on a heatproof pan. Broil the chicken as close to the heat source as possible for 5 to 7 minutes.
   Carefully turn each piece of chicken over and broil another 5 to 7 minutes or until the chicken is cooked through. Place the chicken on a cutting board and allow to cool. Then cut into bite-size pieces about 3/4

inch square. Place the pieces on a white flat serving dish and surround with watercress leaves. Spear the chicken with bamboo skewers. Serve at room temperature.

PLAN AHEAD

Charred Sesame Chicken can be broiled several hours in advance. Left-over portions can be refrigerated and served at room temperature the following day. Keep in mind that it is crucial to marinate the chicken for 24 hours.

*NOTE

There are many different brands of sesame paste, sometimes called sesame butter, which is actually the Middle Eastern tahini. Sahadi is by far the best brand. When you first open the can in which it is sold, you must place the paste in a blender or food processor, as there is much oil separation. Once this is done, it should be stored in a glass jar in the refrigerator, where it will keep for at least a year.

For the Chinese black tea, you can substitute English or American unscented.

You can make your own Chili Oil or you can use the commercially made brand of your choice.

Sesame Chicken Salad

1–2 medium-size leeks
4 pounds whole chicken
   breasts, weighed with the
   bone and skin
2 tablespoons unhulled
   sesame seeds

DRESSING
1 medium-size garlic clove
1 cup sesame paste*
1/3 cup steeped black Chinese
   tea*

1/4 cup dark soy sauce
11/2 tablespoons Chili Oil*
2 tablespoons Oriental sesame
   oil
2 tablespoons sugar
2 tablespoons red wine
   vinegar
1/2 cup scallions, white and
   green parts, cut into 1/8-inch
   rounds

Leafy lettuce leaves

Serves 4–6

1. Remove the root end of the leeks, then split the leeks in half length-wise all the way through. Place them under forcefully running warm water to remove all traces of sand. Then cut the green part only into 2-inch pieces (reserve the white part for use in other recipes). The yield should be 2 cups cut leeks.

2. Place 2 inches of water in a medium-size saucepan with a tight-fitting cover. Place the leeks on the bottom to serve as a rack for the chicken. Bring the water to a boil. Add the chicken breasts. Cover, then turn the heat to low, and simmer the chicken breasts for 30 minutes. Remove the chicken from its broth (reserve the broth for another recipe). Allow the chicken to drain and cool in a strainer over a bowl.

3. While the chicken is cooling, dry-cook the unhulled sesame seeds in an iron skillet over low heat, until they begin to brown. Remove them to a plate.

4. When the chicken is cool, shred it with your fingers, which will make the chicken pieces more porous and better able to absorb the dressing.

5. Mix together the ingredients for the dressing, ideally in a food processor. If using a food processor, add the garlic clove first. After it is minced, add the remaining dressing ingredients except for the scallions. Process until smooth.

6. Place the chicken and the scallions in a bowl. Add the dressing and mix well. Place the Sesame Chicken Salad on a bed of lettuce on a serving platter. Sprinkle with sesame seeds. Serve at room temperature.

PLAN AHEAD

The chicken breasts can be poached a day in advance, cooked and shredded, covered well, and placed in the refrigerator. The ingredients for the dressing can be combined a day in advance, but optimally speaking, the garlic and the scallions should be added to the dressing the same day. The chicken and the dressing can be combined several hours in advance and refrigerated. Allow to become room temperature before serving.

*NOTE

There are many different brands of sesame paste, sometimes called sesame butter, which is actually the Middle Eastern tahini. Sahadi is by far the best brand. When you first open the can in which it is sold, you must place the paste in a blender or food processor, as there is much oil separation. Once this is done, it should be stored in a glass jar in the refrigerator, where it will keep for at least a year.

For the Chinese black tea, you can substitute English or American unscented.

You can make your own Chili Oil or you can use the commercially made brand of your choice.

Chicken and Garlic Salad

I have made this traditional Chinese chicken entree into an unusual and delicious spicy chicken salad. The rest of the meal does not have to be restricted to Oriental selections.

1 pound boneless, skinless, chicken breast

MARINADE
1 tablespoon cornstarch
1 tablespoon medium-dry sherry
1 egg white

SEASONING SAUCE
1 teaspoon cornstarch dissolved in:
2 tablespoons medium-dry sherry
1 tablespoon dark soy sauce
1 tablespoon light soy sauce
1 tablespoon Chicken Stock
1 teaspoon Hot Sauce*
2 teaspoons sugar
2 teaspoons red wine vinegar

1 cup peanut oil for deep-frying

1 tablespoon minced garlic
2 teaspoons fresh, minced ginger
1/2 cup diced red sweet pepper
1/2 cup scallions, white and green parts included, cut into thin strips
3/4 cup unpeeled zucchini, cut into julienne strips

1 teaspoon Oriental sesame oil

6–8 lettuce leaves

Serves 6–8

1. Partially freeze the chicken breast, then cut into thin strips about 3 inches long. This is done by first slicing the chicken breasts then piling the slices on top of one another and slicing again into thin, matchlike strips about 3 inches long.

2. In a medium-size bowl, combine the ingredients for the marinade. Add the chicken to the marinade and stir well. Place the chicken in the refrigerator for at least 1 hour, or up to 12 hours.

3. In a small bowl, combine the ingredients for the seasoning sauce.

4. Place a steel wok or iron skillet over high heat for about 2 minutes or until it starts to smoke. Add the peanut oil and heat until you see waves or it reaches 325°. Restir the chicken in the marinade and add it to the wok all at once, stirring in a circular motion for about 1 minute, or until the chicken turns opaque. Pour the chicken and the oil into a colander set over a bowl. Shake the colander to aid the draining.

5. Do not wash the wok. Return the wok to high heat and add the garlic and ginger, stirring for a few seconds. Then add the peppers, scallions,

and zucchini. Stir-fry for about 1 to 2 minutes or until the vegetables begin to soften.

6. Restir the seasoning sauce and add it to the wok all at once, along with the chicken, continuing to stir-fry until all the ingredients have been well combined. Turn off the heat. Add the sesame oil, mix again, and empty the contents of the wok onto a plate and allow to cool. When cool, divide the chicken mixture into 6 to 8 portions. Place each portion on a lettuce leaf.

PLAN AHEAD

Chicken and Garlic Salad can be made early in the day or a day in advance. It should be served at room temperature.

*NOTE

For the Hot Sauce you can substitute ¼ teaspoon Tabasco sauce.

Scallop and Ginger Salad

I can't tell you how much leftover Chinese food I have eaten in my life. Knowing that Chinese food should never be rewarmed, as the vegetables will become soggy and the meat will be overcooked, I always eat it at room temperature. One day I put some leftover Scallops in Ginger Sauce on a bed of lettuce leaves and had a great salad. The following dish is traditionally served hot, but if made a few hours in advance and allowed to cool to room temperature, it becomes an exciting salad with characteristic Chinese tastes and textures.

1 pound bay scallops

MARINADE
1 egg white
1 tablespoon cornstarch
1 tablespoon medium-dry
  sherry

SEASONING SAUCE
1 teaspoon cornstarch
  dissolved in:
2 tablespoons medium-dry
  sherry
1½ tablespoons dark soy
  sauce
1 teaspoon red wine vinegar
1 teaspoon sugar
1 tablespoon Chicken Stock
1 tablespoon Glace de
  Viande*
1 teaspoon Hot Sauce*

1 cup peanut oil
2 tablespoons shredded winter
  ginger *or* ¼ cup shredded
  spring ginger
2 scallions, white and green
  parts, cut in ¼-inch rounds
1 teaspoon minced garlic
½ cup triangle-cut red sweet
  pepper
½ cup strung and slant-cut
  snow peas
½ cup water chestnuts, sliced
  in rounds
2 teaspoons Oriental sesame
  oil

Lettuce leaves

Serves 4–6

1. Rinse the scallops, then drain in a strainer set over a bowl for about 15 minutes. Place the drained scallops on several layers of paper towels. Go over each one very carefully and remove any particles of sand or shell.
2. Place the ingredients for the marinade in a bowl and mix well.
Add the scallops to the marinade and stir well until they are coated. Place the scallops in the refrigerator and marinate for at least 1 hour or up to 12 hours.
3. Combine the ingredients for the seasoning sauce.
4. Place a wok over high heat until it smokes. This will take about 2

minutes. Add the peanut oil and heat until it reaches 325° or until you see waves.

5. Restir the scallops in the marinade. Holding the scallops near the wok, add them all at once, stirring with a pair of chopsticks in a circular motion for about 1 minute or until the scallops turn white. Turn off the heat and pour out the oil and the scallops into a colander set over a bowl. Shake the colander to aid the draining. Make sure the colander is not sitting in the oil. Do not wash the wok.

6. Return the wok to high heat. In the oil that glazes the wok, stir-fry the ginger, scallions, garlic, and red peppers for 1 minute.

Return the scallops to the wok, along with the snow peas and water chestnuts. Mix briefly.

7. Restir the seasoning sauce. Add it all at once to the wok; stir-fry about 30 seconds or until the sauce has thickened. Turn off the heat. Add the sesame oil. Mix a few seconds. Empty the contents of the wok onto a plate. Allow to cool. Serve individual portions in lettuce leaves.

PLAN AHEAD

Scallop and Ginger Salad is best when made several hours in advance and served at room temperature.

*NOTE

You can make your own Glace de Viande or in some areas you can purchase it. It is also possible to make this dish successfully without it.

For the Hot Sauce you can substitute ¼ teaspoon Tabasco sauce.

Cauliflower with
Oriental Vinaigrette Dressing

East meets West in a salad that combines an American vegetable with an Oriental version of classic French vinaigrette. Besides cauliflower, I love to serve this dressing over many different types of steamed vegetables, such as asparagus, string beans, or broccoli.

1 large head cauliflower

ORIENTAL VINAIGRETTE DRESSING
1/2 cup chopped red sweet pepper
1/4 cup scallions, white and green parts included, cut into 1/8-inch rounds
1 teaspoon minced garlic
11/2 tablespoons Oriental sesame oil

11/2 tablespoons peanut oil
3 tablespoons light soy sauce
2 teaspoons sugar
3 tablespoons red wine vinegar
1 teaspoon Hot Sauce*

GARNISH
1 tablespoon unhulled sesame seeds

Serves 6–10

1. Separate the cauliflower florets, then steam them for 8 to 10 minutes or until tender. Remove them from the heat source and place the florets into a large bowl filled with ice water. Cool briefly, then drain. Place the florets on a platter.

2. Combine all the Oriental Vinaigrette Dressing ingredients in a bowl. Stir well.

3. Place the cauliflower florets on a flat serving dish, pour the dressing over them, then sprinkle with sesame seeds. Serve immediately.

PLAN AHEAD
Step 1 can be done a day in advance, in which case place the cauliflower in the refrigerator.

Step 2 can be prepared several hours in advance.

*NOTE
For the Hot Sauce you can substitute 1/4 teaspoon Tabasco sauce.

Turkish Rice Salad

1/2 cup pine nuts
2 tablespoons butter
1 cup chopped onions
Salt to taste
Freshly ground black pepper
 (20 turns of the mill)
3 tablespoons curry powder
2 cups raw long-grain rice,
 rinsed and drained
2 1/2 cups Chicken Stock
1/2 cup currants
1/2 cup white raisins
1/2 cup chopped carrots,
 scrubbed but not peeled

1/2 cup chopped green bell
 pepper
1/2 cup chopped red sweet
 pepper
1/2 cup sliced black olives
2 tablespoons chopped parsley

DRESSING
1 teaspoon salt
2 tablespoons lemon juice
2 teaspoons Dijon mustard
Freshly ground black pepper
 (10 turns of the mill)
6 tablespoons olive oil

Serves 8–10

1. Preheat the oven to 325°. Place the pine nuts on an ungreased cookie sheet or an iron skillet and roast for 5 to 10 minutes or until they are golden brown. Allow to cool.

2. In a 2 to 3-quart saucepan melt the butter until it foams. Add the onions and sauté over medium heat 2 to 3 minutes or until they are translucent.

Add the salt, pepper, and curry powder; stir briefly. This brief cooking will bring out the flavor of the curry powder.

Add the rice and stir until it is well combined with the curry powder.

Add the chicken stock and turn the heat to high. Bring the chicken stock to a rapid boil, stirring well in a figure-8 motion with chopsticks or a wooden spoon. Turn the heat to low, cover, and cook the rice for 15 minutes. Turn off the heat. If using an electric range, remove from the heat source.

Uncover and add the currants and the raisins. Do not stir. Return the cover and allow the rice to relax for 10 minutes.

Uncover the rice again; add the carrots and the green and red peppers. Do not stir. Cover and allow to relax for another 10 minutes.

Remove the cover and add the olives and chopped parsley; mix well. Empty the rice into a large bowl.

3. Dissolve the salt in the lemon juice. Add the mustard, pepper, and olive oil. Stir well.

Add the dressing and the pine nuts to the rice mixture. Stir well to combine. Transfer to a serving bowl. Serve at room temperature.

Shrimp and Ham Fried Rice

Fried rice is more special to Americans than to the Chinese, possibly because rice is the staple of the Chinese diet, with the exception of the North where noodles are the staple. Rice is 80 percent of the Chinese food intake. The average person consumes about two pounds of rice a day. In fact, they consider it the main part of their meal and all the other dishes are placed on the table to "season the rice." In China a common greeting is "Have you eaten?" or literally translated, "Have you had rice?" Consequently they frequently have leftover rice which they turn into fried rice.

The secret to successful fried rice is to start with leftover or thoroughly cooked and cooled white rice. The Chinese would never add soy sauce to season their fried rice as they consider it a class distinction to eat white rice. They would also serve it hot but I am suggesting it as a room-temperature dish, the way the French would serve a rice salad.

1½ cups raw long-grain rice, rinsed and drained
5 tablespoons peanut oil
2 slightly beaten eggs
1 cup mung bean sprouts

SEASONING SAUCE
1 tablespoon dark soy sauce
1 tablespoon oyster sauce
½ teaspoon sugar

⅓ cup scallions, white and green parts included, cut in ⅛-inch rounds
½ cup diced red sweet pepper or yellow Holland pepper
½ cup diced unpeeled zucchini
1 cup diced cooked shrimp*
1 cup diced smoked ham

Serves 6–8

1. Place 1½ cups rice in an enamel saucepan with a tight-fitting cover. Add 2¼ cups cold water. Bring to a rapid boil. Stir with a wooden spoon. Cover and turn the heat to the lowest possible setting and cook 15 minutes or until all the water has evaporated. When this happens, you will see little holes in the top of the rice. The Chinese call them fish eyes. Turn off the heat and allow the rice to relax for 20 minutes. At the end of the relaxing period, remove the cover and empty the rice into a large bowl, stirring gently to break up the grains. This will yield 3 cups cooked rice. Refrigerate the rice for several hours.

2. Place a 12-inch iron skillet over high heat for about 1 minute. Add 1 tablespoon of the peanut oil. While the oil is heating, rotate the skillet above the heat so the oil is evenly distributed. Pour off the excess oil and reserve. Add the eggs all at once. Then turn the heat to medium. Rotate the skillet so that a large thin pancake is formed. Remove the egg pancake

by inverting the skillet on a flat surface. Allow the pancake to cool, then dice.

3. Place a 14-inch steel wok over high heat for about 2 minutes. Do not add oil. Add the bean sprouts and cook, shaking the wok occasionally until they are scorched, which will take about 2 minutes. Flip and scorch on other side. Remove the bean sprouts from the wok and reserve.

4. Combine the ingredients for the seasoning sauce.

5. Heat 1 tablespoon of the oil in the wok. Stir-fry the scallions, red or yellow pepper, and zucchini for about 1 minute. Remove the vegetables from the wok.

6. In the remaining 3 tablespoons of oil, stir-fry the cold rice over high heat for 2 to 3 minutes, pressing down with a steel spatula to scorch the rice where possible.

Add the seasoning sauce and continue to stir-fry until the rice is brown.

Add the shrimp, ham, diced eggs, bean sprouts, scallions, red or yellow pepper, and zucchini. Stir-fry 1 more minute or until all the ingredients have been thoroughly mixed together. Serve hot or at room temperature.

*NOTE

For the shrimp you can substitute crabmeat or lobster.

Wild Rice Salad

Wild rice is not actually rice but a distant cousin. It is a grain, the seeds of a wild grass that is not wild anymore.

Americans always liked wild rice. The Indians used to harvest it from their canoes. Presently two thirds of the world's supply comes from Minnesota, Michigan, and Wisconsin, where it grows in abundance in shallow lakes and swamps. Ducks and other game birds feed on it, and it is frequently found as a major ingredient in the stuffing of a bird or as an accompaniment to roast poultry. This recipe gives it a new role. Its distinctive nutty flavor enhances this room-temperature rice salad.

1/2 cup slivered almonds
1 cup raw wild rice
2 tablespoons butter
1/3 cup minced shallots
2 cups Chicken Stock
Salt to taste

Freshly ground black pepper
(10 turns of the mill)
1 pound unshelled fresh peas*
1 cup sliced mushrooms
1/2 cup sour cream
2 tablespoons chopped parsley

Serves 8–10

1. Preheat the oven to 325° and roast the almonds on a cookie sheet or in an iron skillet for 10 minutes or until they are golden brown.

2. Place the wild rice in a strainer and rinse very well under forcefully running water. Allow to drain.

3. In a 1 1/2 to 2-quart saucepan melt the butter until it foams. Add the shallots and stir briefly.

Add the wild rice and stir with a wooden spoon for about a minute or until the rice is coated with the butter.

Turn the heat to high and add the chicken stock, salt, and pepper. Bring the rice to a rapid boil, stirring well in a figure-8 motion with chopsticks or a wooden spoon. Turn the heat to low, cover, and simmer 1 to 1 1/4 hours.

4. Just before the rice has absorbed all the chicken stock, stir in the peas. Cook for 5 minutes.

Remove the cover. Add the mushrooms, sour cream, and parsley. Mix well.

5. Transfer the rice to a serving bowl. When it has cooled, stir in the slivered almonds. Serve Wild Rice Salad at room temperature.

PLAN AHEAD

Wild Rice Salad is best when made several hours in advance and served at room temperature. However, it can be made several days in advance. Remove it from the refrigerator about 2 hours before serving.

*NOTE

For the fresh peas, you can substitute 1 cup frozen peas, in which case add the defrosted peas when you add the mushrooms, sour cream, and parsley.

Bulgur Wheat Pilaf

3/4 cup pine nuts
3 cups Chicken Stock
2 1/2 cups bulgur wheat
1/4 cup shredded orange zest
1/2 cup dried currants
2 tablespoons butter
1/2 cup diced carrot
1 cup scallions, white and green parts included, cut into 1/8-inch rounds

1 cup strung and diced snow peas*
1/2 cup chopped parsley
2 1/2 tablespoons lemon juice
1/2 cup fresh orange juice
1/4 cup olive oil
1 tablespoon dark soy sauce
1 cup pecans
1 cup walnuts

Serves 20

1. Preheat the oven to 325°. Place the pine nuts on an ungreased cookie sheet. Roast them for approximately 5 to 10 minutes or until they are golden brown.

2. In a heavy enamel pot with a tight-fitting cover, bring the stock to a rolling boil.

3. While the stock is heating, place the bulgur wheat in a strainer. Rinse under cold running water, then drain. Add the bulgur wheat to the boiling stock. Stir a few seconds. Cover, turn the heat to low and cook for 20 minutes.

Turn off the heat, add the orange zest and currants. Replace the cover and let the bulgur wheat relax for 30 minutes. During the relaxing period, the orange zest and currants will soften.

4. In a 10-inch skillet, heat the butter until it foams. Add the carrots; sauté over low heat for about 1 minute or until the carrots slightly soften.

Add the scallions and the snow peas; sauté for another 30 seconds.

5. After the 30-minute relaxing period of the bulgur wheat, remove the cover. Add the parsley, lemon juice, orange juice, olive oil, soy sauce, the sautéed vegetables, the roasted pine nuts, along with the raw pecans and raw walnuts. Stir well and serve at room temperature.

PLAN AHEAD
Bulgur Wheat Pilaf will last for 5 days in the refrigerator.

*NOTE
For the snow peas you can substitute 1 cup frozen green peas, defrosted.

Tortellini Vegetable Salad with Ham

1/4 cup diced carrots,
   scrubbed but not peeled

1/2 pound fresh tortellini
2 teaspoons salt

2 tablespoons olive oil
1 teaspoon minced garlic
1/4 cup diced roasted peppers,
   from a jar

1 tablespoon roasted pepper
   juice, from the jar
1/2 cup diced baked ham
1/4 cup diced unpeeled
   zucchini
1/4 cup diced unpeeled yellow
   squash
1/4 cup chopped fresh dill
Freshly ground black pepper
   (15 turns of the mill)

Serves 4–6

1. Bring a large kettle of water to a rolling boil. Add the carrots and blanch for 1 minute. Remove the carrots from the water with a slotted spoon.

Return the water to a rolling boil. Add the tortellini and salt; cook until tender but firm (about 5 minutes). Drain in a colander.

Place the carrots and the tortellini in a bowl.

2. Heat the olive oil in a small sauté skillet until it is hot. Sauté the garlic over a low heat for about 1 minute or until it is lightly browned. Remove from the heat source. Add the garlic to the tortellini, along with the roasted peppers, roasted pepper juice, ham, zucchini, yellow squash, dill, and pepper. Fold and mix well. Serve at room temperature.

PLAN AHEAD

The entire dish can be prepared several hours in advance. Leftovers should be refrigerated and allowed to come to room temperature before serving.

Greek Pasta Salad

2 teaspoons salt
1 pound dried fusilli

1/2 cup olive oil
1 teaspoon red wine vinegar
1 teaspoon dried oregano
1/2 cup chopped parsley
1 tablespoon salt
Freshly ground black pepper
(20 turns of the mill)

1 cup sliced purple onion
1 cup diced cucumber (small gherkin)
1 cup diced combined green bell and red sweet peppers
1 small jar marinated artichoke hearts, rinsed and drained
3/4 cup black Greek olives
11/2 cups cubed feta cheese

Serves 12–15

1. Bring a large kettle of salted water to a rolling boil. Add the fusilli and cook until tender but firm, about 9 to 10 minutes. Drain in a colander.
2. Place the fusilli and all the remaining ingredients in a large bowl. Toss until well combined. Serve at room temperature.

PLAN AHEAD

Greek Pasta Salad can be made early in the day and served at room temperature.

It stores well in the refrigerator for at least 2 or 3 days.

Conchiglie Salad

Conchiglie means seashells and this short concave pasta looks like an open scallop shell. It is often used for cheese-based sauces because the shape grips a thick, creamy sauce beautifully. You can buy smooth or ridged conchiglie.

2 teaspoons salt
1 pound dried conchiglie

3 cups chopped celery
1 1/2 cups scallions, white and green parts included, cut in 1/8-inch rounds
1 cup sliced radishes
1/2 cup chopped parsley
2 cups mayonnaise

3 tablespoons red wine vinegar
1 tablespoon balsamic vinegar
1 1/2 tablespoons Pommery mustard
1 teaspoon celery seeds
1 teaspoon salt
Freshly ground black pepper (20 turns of the mill)
2 cups coarsely grated English Farm House Cheddar cheese

Serves 6–8

1. Bring a large kettle of salted water to a rolling boil. Add the conchiglie and cook for about 10 minutes. Drain in a colander. Place under cold running water, then drain again.

2. Combine all the ingredients except the conchiglie in a bowl. Mix well, then gently stir in the pasta. Refrigerate until serving.

PLAN AHEAD

The entire salad can be prepared a day in advance.

Fusilli with Pesto

Fusilli is pasta shaped like a spring. It's a fun pasta that gives a great look to a salad. The flavorful bits of the sauce are captured in the spiral shapes.

1 teaspoon salt	**1 clove garlic, minced**
1/2 pound dried fusilli	**1/2 cup freshly grated Parmesan cheese**
1/2 bunch watercress	**1 cup diced Doux de**
1/2 cup Pesto Base*	**Montagne cheese***
1 teaspoon salt	**1/4 cup shredded prosciutto**
Freshly ground black pepper (10 turns of the mill)	

Serves 4–6

1. Bring a large kettle of salted water to a rolling boil. Add the fusilli and cook until tender but firm, about 9 to 10 minutes. Drain in a colander.
2. While the fusilli is cooking, cut off at least 3 inches of the watercress stem (while it is still tied in a bunch). Wash, drain, and spin-dry.
3. Place the fusilli in a serving bowl. While the fusilli is still warm, add the pesto base, 1 teaspoon salt, pepper, garlic and the Parmesan cheese. Toss well with a wooden spatula.
4. Add the Doux de Montagne, watercress, and prosciutto. Toss until all the ingredients have been thoroughly combined. Serve at room temperature.

PLAN AHEAD

This room-temperature pasta dish can be made early in the day.

*NOTE

Preferably use fresh Pesto Base rather than frozen.

For the Doux de Montagne, you can substitute another semisoft, mild cheese.

Orzo with Broccoli and Pesto

This is a great little side dish I love to serve as a substitute for rice or potatoes. It goes beautifully with grilled fish, hamburger, roast chicken, or veal chops.

1/4 **cup pine nuts**	3/4 **cup chopped smoked ham**
	2 **tablespoons chopped parsley**
2 **teaspoons salt**	2 **tablespoons Pesto Base***
1/2 **pound dried orzo**	**Freshly ground black pepper**
	(20 turns of the mill)
2 **cups broccoli florets**	1/2 **cup grated Parmesan**
5 **tablespoons olive oil**	**cheese**
1 **tablespoon minced garlic**	

Serves 4–6

1. Preheat the oven to 325°. Roast the pine nuts on an ungreased cookie sheet or in an iron skillet for 5 to 10 minutes or until they are golden brown. Allow to cool.

2. Bring a large kettle of salted water to a rolling boil. Add the orzo and cook until tender but firm, about 5 minutes. Using a strainer, remove the orzo from the boiling water. Allow to drain.

3. Return the water to a boil. Add the broccoli florets and blanch for about 3 minutes. Drain the broccoli, then plunge it into ice-cold water. This will stop the cooking and hold the color. Drain again. Dry well.

4. In a 10-inch skillet heat the olive oil. Add the garlic. Sauté over low heat for about 1 minute or until the garlic is lightly browned.

Add the ham, parsley, and drained orzo; stir well for about 1 minute. Add the pesto base, black pepper, and broccoli; toss well for another minute. Turn off the heat.

Add the Parmesan cheese and pine nuts. Continue to toss until all the ingredients are well combined. Serve at room temperature.

PLAN AHEAD

Orzo with Broccoli and Pesto can be made several hours in advance.

*NOTE

Preferably use fresh Pesto Base as opposed to frozen. For the Pesto Base, you can substitute 3/4 cup fresh chopped basil.

Pastas

Everybody Loves it

Pasta is the food everyone loves, and the pasta sauces you'll find here are a precious collection that I hope will bring you as much pleasure as they have brought me and my students.

In Italy pasta is the star, not the sauce, and rightly so. Italian hand-rolled, homemade pasta has an incredibly delicate texture and taste. The function of the sauce is to season the pasta itself. As I do not pretend to be a master of the art of pasta-making, I have made the sauce the star. And for the busy working person, I believe it is more realistic to tackle only the sauces. It is too time-consuming, given our hectic schedules, to make the pasta as well as the sauce.

Certain sauces, such as those containing cream, form a natural bond with fresh pasta, whereas most tomato-based sauces go well with dried pasta. When fresh is called for, I suggest purchasing a good local brand, one which is not pasty. Although there are pasta suggestions with each recipe, using fresh or dried is the reader's choice.

Whichever you are using, keep in mind that the amount of minutes it takes to boil the pasta to an al dente state (to the tooth, literally; meaning, figuratively, until it is tender but firm) will depend on what type of pasta you are using. Dried pasta takes between five and ten minutes to boil, according to its thickness. Fresh pasta takes a considerably shorter time, between two and four minutes. Because fresh pasta has a softer consistency, it can never be cooked al dente.

When it comes to the actual sauces, you will find that many of them can function with pasta as a first course, the way you would expect to eat in an Italian restaurant—especially the ones with shellfish. A soup and salad would complete the meal. Some work best as a side dish, like Fettucine with Marsala and Porcini, or Orzo Primavera, which is perfect for a room-temperature buffet with many assorted salads. The heartiest pasta dishes have meat-based sauces, like Veal Ragoût, Red-cooked Shoulder of Pork, or Porcini Veal Sauce. Begin or end this type of meal with a light, lettuce-based salad.

These pastas will arouse the curiosity of your most sophisticated guest. There is the unique combination of a French liqueur, an Indian spice, and an Italian vegetable found in Pasta with Saffron, Lobster, and Fennel. There are the variations on the classics, like Linguini with Maraciara Sauce, a subtle clam dish with a touch of tomato; or Spaghetti with Puttanesca Sauce, in which caviar takes the place of anchovies. There are pastas such as Spaghetti with

Salsa Forte and Chinese Pepper Pasta that feature Chinese leftover vegetable dishes. And some are a combining of Chinese techniques with Italian or French seasoning, as in Pasta with Spring Vegetables and Crème Fraîche.

As I began to experiment with pasta sauces, many of them Italian-based, I was amazed to find how many similarities there are between the two cuisines. Both cuisines feature not a large main dish but rather many courses; nothing can be more economical than a Chinese meal or an Italian pasta sauce; and they both frequently use a little bit of ham to season a dish. When it comes to the preparation and cooking of these pasta sauces, I also apply the same principles as I do for Chinese cooking. All the ingredients are chopped ahead, and I organize the numerous seasonings in dishes on a tray before I begin to cook.

Pasta Pantry

The secret of making spur-of-the-moment pasta dishes is a well-stocked larder. Pasta sauces are a category that begs the cook to be inventive. Pasta can so easily be a foil for leftovers, make a seasonal item shine, stretch one lobster to feed four, turn a main ingredient into a seasoning. Once you set up your pasta pantry, I encourage you not only to make these recipes but also to create your own. By keeping certain staples on hand, you can always make impromptu sauces.

I am never without a jar of sun-dried tomatoes, olive paste, olive oil, garlic, and shallots. For eleven months out of the year, I have cans of tomatoes from the San Marzano region of Italy, and for four to six weeks in the summer, I have fresh, ripening tomatoes with their wonderful flavor and consistency. I keep dried porcini mushrooms, saffron, unsalted butter, cream, and Parmigiano-Reggiano cheese, along with fresh pasta and a box or two of De Cecco pasta.

When I am creating a pasta sauce, I go to the store to buy fresh ingredients. I look for a local vegetable that is at its peak. I taste the mascarpone to determine if it is fresh; if so, I buy a small portion to use instead of cream. If fresh herbs are available, I get some basil, chives, and Italian flat parsley. And of course a little prosciutto.

Pasta Equipment

Why is it that when you eat pasta in a restaurant, it is always steaming hot and when you have it at home, it never is? Your plates should be warmed in a 250-degree oven and so should the serving platter if you are using one.

My favorite serving platter is the skillet. I cook and serve most hot pasta dishes in the same skillet. If you are purchasing one, buy heavy-gauged stainless steel, copper, or enamel. They each look good, stay hot, and keep the pasta hot.

Equipment other than the 10 to 12-inch sauté skillet includes one or two stainless-steel or enamel pots. They should be large enough to boil water for the pasta, 4 to 5 quarts. While the pasta is boiling, it is helpful to have a spaghetti fork with pegs for lifting it out of the water to see if it is al dente. *After this, a colander is needed for draining, a wooden spoon to stir the sauce, and a wooden spatula to get all the sauce out of the skillet.*

For cutting the various ingredients, you will need a chef's knife or cleaver, a paring knife, and a wooden chopping block. For mincing, you might like a minichop for small quantities of garlic or fresh herbs or a food processor for larger quantities.

Because you can freeze many of these sauces and serve them at the last minute, you will also need wide-mouthed glass jars, which should be filled only to two thirds of capacity to allow for expansion in the freezer. Many of the sauces also keep well for days in a glass jar in the refrigerator. As for the pasta itself, the fresh can be frozen for one month (but is not as good) or can be refrigerated in a plastic bag for two days. Dried pasta keeps well on the shelf for at least six months.

I would like to emphasize to you the PLAN AHEAD *aspect of making these dishes. Some sauces can be frozen and others can be made early in the day. You merely turn off the heat, put the sauce away, and, when ready to use, boil the pasta and reheat the sauce.*

Tomato Sauce

This basic tomato sauce has become a staple I use with many cuisines. It is great to have on hand for French or Spanish cooking when a recipe calls for a few tablespoons of tomato sauce. I use it in Chinese cooking instead of the catsup which so many Chinese chefs use and in Italian cooking as a base for many pasta sauces.

The original recipe came from Lydie Marshall, who makes some of the best French food I have ever eaten. Acting on a recommendation by Giuliano Bugialli, the well-known author and teacher of Italian cooking, that adding the green part of the leek imparts a great flavor to tomato sauce, I tried it and emphatically agreed.

In the summertime and early fall, I use well-ripened fresh, local tomatoes. At all other times of the year, I use any good-quality canned tomato from the San Marzano region of Italy. It will say San Marzano on the label, and to me the region is more important than the brand. Because this sauce does not have any added herbs, it can be used in many dishes. I make it up in big batches (never big enough, as it goes so fast), and freeze it in small glass jars, filled two-thirds full to allow for expansion. I don't use plastic for storing anything, as I believe it imparts a flavor and glass does not. Wide-mouthed jars are valuable for storing many things, so start saving them now.

4 cups canned Italian tomatoes (measured with their juice)* or 3 pounds very ripe fresh tomatoes*	**2 tablespoons butter**
	1 tablespoon minced garlic
	1 teaspoon sugar
	Salt to taste
1 medium-size leek	**Freshly ground black pepper**
2 tablespoons olive oil	**(20 turns of the mill)**

Yield 3 cups

1. If using canned tomatoes, pass the tomatoes through a food mill into a bowl. Reserve the puréed tomatoes with their juice; discard the seeds. If using fresh tomatoes, dice them without peeling or seeding.

2. Remove the root end of the leek, then split the leek in half lengthwise all the way through. Place it under forcefully running warm water to remove all traces of sand. Mince the green part only (reserve the white part for use in other recipes). The yield should be 1 cup minced leeks.

3. In a 12-inch skillet, heat the olive oil and butter until the butter foams. Add the leeks and garlic; sauté over medium-low heat for about 5 minutes or until the leeks are limp. Add the tomatoes, sugar, salt, and pepper. Bring to a simmer over high heat. Stir well to combine. Turn the heat to low.

4. Simmer uncovered for ¾ hour, or until the sauce has reduced by

half. If using fresh tomatoes, pass the sauce through the food mill.

5. Cool, then place in small covered glass jars.

PLAN AHEAD

Refrigerated, the sauce will keep for 1 week. Freeze the sauce for long-term storage (up to 6 months). Fill the jar two-thirds full to avoid breakage when the sauce expands.

*NOTE

Four cups canned Italian tomatoes are contained in one 35-ounce tin. If you are using fresh tomatoes, buy them several days or even a week in advance so they will properly ripen. I have found that—except for a few months in the summer—good-quality canned tomatoes produce a better sauce.

Hot Sauce

One day out of the blue Madame Chu invited me over to taste Madame Koo's Hot Sauce. Madame Chu was the first person to teach Chinese cooking in America and is the author of several Chinese cookbooks. She is the woman from whom I originally learned Chinese cooking, and to whom I eventually became apprenticed.

It was the early 1970's and I was just learning about Sichuan cooking at the time. Hot Sauce, also called chili paste, is a major seasoning and reason for the heat in Sichuan cooking. I had been buying a mass-produced locally available brand in New York City's Chinatown. When I tasted Madame Koo's Hot Sauce, I couldn't believe the difference in quality and taste. Her homemade sauce had many layers of flavor, not just hot and spicy. I began buying it at her little take-out restaurant and recommending it to my students, who also flocked there to buy this little-known treasure. Then all of a sudden Madame Koo went out of business and her Hot Sauce vanished, never to be seen again. I guarded my last jar in hopes of reproducing the sauce on my own. I created each new batch with the help of my students, sniffing and tasting against the only remaining jar I had. Finally, after a year of trying, I obtained the taste and texture I was after.

This is a Hot Sauce that you can apply to all cuisines, not just Chinese. It can be used in a Mexican chili, an Italian diavolo sauce, an Indian curry, and more. My students put it on open-faced melted cheese sandwiches, in a meat loaf, in vegetable soup—any time they want to make a dish spicy. At this point in my culinary career, I don't think I could cook without it.

CHILI OIL
3/4 cup olive oil
1/3 cup ground dried chili peppers

1 medium-size green bell pepper
2 medium-size red sweet peppers

10–12 cloves of garlic
1 4-ounce jar whole roasted peppers
3 tablespoons olive oil
2 teaspoons sugar
2 teaspoons red wine vinegar
1 teaspoon balsamic vinegar

Yield approximately 2 cups

1. *To make the chili oil:* Place a small wok or iron skillet over high heat for about 1 minute or until it starts to smoke. Add the 3/4 cup of olive oil and heat over a low setting for about 3 or 4 minutes or until you see waves (350°). Turn off the heat and wait 1 minute. So that it will cook evenly, add

the ground dried chili peppers all at once. Stir briefly and allow to cool ½ hour.

2. Cut the red and green peppers in half. Remove the seeds and membrane. Then dice the peppers into approximately ½-inch pieces. Place the diced pepper in the container of a food processor. Turn the machine on and off until they are minced. Remove the peppers from the bowl of the food processor.

3. Crush the garlic cloves and remove the skin. Turn the food processor on, put the garlic cloves through the feeding tube, and turn the machine on and off until the garlic is finely minced. Remove from processor.

4. Place the contents of the jar of roasted peppers in the processor and purée.

5. Place another wok or sauté skillet over high heat for about 1 minute. Add the 3 tablespoons of olive oil. Turn the heat to low and add the minced garlic. Sauté the garlic for 2 to 3 minutes or until it starts to brown.

Add the minced red and green peppers. Turn the heat to high and sauté for another 2 to 3 minutes or until the peppers soften. Turn the heat to medium low and continue to cook for another 10 minutes or until all the juice from the peppers has evaporated.

6. Turn off the heat. Add the sugar, vinegars, puréed roasted peppers, and all the cooled chili oil including the chili peppers that have settled to the bottom. Stir very well. Allow to cool, then place in small glass jars with tight-fitting covers and refrigerate.

PLAN AHEAD

Hot Sauce can be stored in the refrigerator for up to six months or more.

*NOTE

Always stir the Hot Sauce well before measuring with a clean spoon. Never leave the Hot Sauce out at room temperature. Use small jars as opposed to one large jar, so that it will store for a longer time. If mold or bubbling occurs, discard. The amount you add to various dishes depends on the taste of you and your guests. Usually ½ to 2 teaspoons is enough to make one single recipe spicy.

Pesto Base

There are certain invaluable staples on which I have become dependent. Pesto base is one of them. It is a means of storing fresh basil to preserve its flavor. Pesto base is not to be confused with pesto sauce, which is made by grinding together not only fresh basil and olive oil, but also garlic, pine nuts, and cheese.

In the summertime when fresh basil with all its aroma is at its peak, I make pesto base, put it in small glass jars, and freeze it for use all year long. I find it to be a wonderful addition not only to pasta dishes but also as a flavoring for soups and salad dressings.

5 cups basil leaves
1/2 cup olive oil

Yield 1 cup

1. Wash and spin-dry the basil leaves.
2. Place the basil leaves and oil in the bowl of a food processor. Turn on and off until mixture is finely chopped.

PLAN AHEAD

Pesto base can be stored in a covered glass jar in the refrigerator for several months or frozen for 1 year. It is best to top the pesto base with a half-inch layer of olive oil. If freezing, freeze in small quantities, such as tablespoons, quarter cup, and half cup.

Tortellini with Creamy Tomato Sauce

Tomato Sauce and Pesto Base are two staples which stay year-round in my refrigerator. If you have these two ingredients at your finger-tips, Creamy Tomato Sauce is quick and easy. It is excellent served with any kind of filled pasta such as tortellini, tortelloni, ravioli, or cappelletti. It can also be served over spaghetti and other pasta.

1 tablespoon oil
1 tablespoon butter
1 teaspoon minced garlic
1 cup Tomato Sauce*
1/2 teaspoon salt
Freshly ground black pepper
   (10 turns of the mill)
2 tablespoons heavy cream

2 tablespoons mascarpone*
1 tablespoon Pesto Base*

2 teaspoons salt
1/2 pound fresh tortellini

1/4 cup grated Parmesan
   cheese

Serves 2–3

1. In a 10-inch skillet, heat the oil and butter until the butter foams. Add the garlic; sauté over low heat for about 1 minute or until lightly browned.

Add the tomato sauce, the 1/2 teaspoon salt, and the pepper; simmer 1 to 2 minutes.

Turn the heat to low. Add the cream and mascarpone; stir over very low heat until combined.

Add the pesto base; stir a few seconds. Turn off the heat.

WHEN READY TO SERVE
2. Bring a large kettle of salted water to a rolling boil. Add the tortellini. Cook until tender but firm. Drain in a colander.

3. Bring the sauce to a simmer. Add the drained tortellini to the simmering sauce. With the heat on high, stir and toss 1 minute or until the sauce has been well combined with the pasta. Turn off the heat. Add the Parmesan cheese. Mix briefly and serve immediately.

PLAN AHEAD
This sauce can be prepared a day in advance, preferably adding the pesto base at the last moment.

*NOTE
If you haven't made up a batch of your own Tomato Sauce, you can use the commercially made brand of your choice.

If mascarpone is not available, increase the cream to 1/4 cup.

Preferably use fresh Pesto Base rather than frozen.

Spaghetti with
Vegetable Tomato Sauce

I only make this dish in the summer when the fresh tomatoes taste like tomatoes and not plastic. The whole dish, in fact, just cries of the summer.

3 cups diced very ripe fresh tomatoes
2 tablespoons olive oil
1 tablespoon butter
1½ cups sliced Spanish onions
2 tablespoons minced shallots
4 cloves garlic, minced
1 teaspoon salt
Freshly ground black pepper (20 turns of the mill)
1 teaspoon sugar
½ cup shredded sweet red or yellow Holland pepper

½ cup shredded unpeeled zucchini
1 tablespoon oil from sun-dried tomatoes*
¼ cup chopped parsley
½ cup chopped basil leaves*

2 teaspoons salt
½ pound dried spaghetti

½ cup grated Parmesan cheese

Serves 2–4

1. Chop the tomatoes coarsely. Seeding and skinning are not necessary.
2. In a 10-inch skillet, heat the olive oil and butter until the butter foams. Add the onions; sauté over medium heat for 2 to 3 minutes or until they are translucent.

Add the shallots and garlic; sauté another 2 minutes or until the onions and garlic have lightly browned.

Add the tomatoes, salt, pepper and sugar; simmer 20 minutes uncovered, stirring occasionally.

Add the peppers and zucchini; sauté 2 more minutes.

Add the sun-dried-tomato oil, the parsley and basil leaves; turn off the heat.

WHEN READY TO SERVE
3. Bring a large kettle of salted water to a rolling boil. Add the spaghetti. Cook until tender but firm. Drain in a colander.
4. Bring the sauce to a simmer. Add the drained spaghetti to the simmering sauce. With the heat on high, stir and toss 1 minute or until the sauce has been well combined with the spaghetti. Turn off the heat. Add the Parmesan cheese. Mix briefly and serve immediately.

PLAN AHEAD

The sauce can be prepared 5 days in advance and stored in the refrigerator.

*NOTE

For the sun-dried-tomato oil, you can substitute 1 tablespoon butter.

For the basil leaves, you can substitute 1 tablespoon Pesto Base. Preferably use fresh Pesto Base rather than frozen.

Roasted Pepper Pasta

1 medium-size yellow Holland pepper*	1 cup Tomato Sauce*
1 medium-size red sweet pepper*	1/2 teaspoon salt
1 tablespoon olive oil	1 tablespoon chopped parsley
1 tablespoon butter	1/4 cup heavy cream
1 tablespoon minced garlic	1 teaspoon Hot Sauce*
1/4 pound sliced mushrooms	2 teaspoons salt
	1/2 pound dried pasta

Serves 2–3

1. *To roast the peppers: Method 1,* for on top of a gas range: Place the whole peppers directly on the heating element of the stove. Turn the heat to low. Roast the peppers, occasionally turning with tongs as the skins begin to char. Keep turning until the entire pepper has charred—the more charred, the easier it will be to peel. Using the lowest possible heat, this will take about 20 to 30 minutes. The yellow pepper will char much more quickly than the red.

Method 2, for the broiling unit, whether gas or electric: Preheat the oven to broil. Place the peppers on a rack resting on a shallow roasting pan or a cookie sheet which has been lined with aluminum foil. Broil the peppers 3 inches from the heat source, turning occasionally. Char all sides of the peppers. This will take from 10 to 20 minutes. The yellow pepper will char much more quickly than the red.

2. Place the charred peppers in a brown paper bag for 10 minutes. Remove the peppers from the paper bag. Quarter them, then core and seed. Using a knife, scrape off the charred skins. Cut the peppers into strips about 1/4-inch wide and reserve.

3. In a 10-inch skillet heat the olive oil and butter until the butter foams. Add the garlic and sauté over low heat until lightly brown.

Add the mushrooms and sauté 1 minute.

Add the roasted peppers, tomato sauce, salt, and parsley; simmer 2 minutes.

Add the cream and Hot Sauce. Stir briefly. Turn off the heat.

4. Bring a large kettle of salted water to a rolling boil. Add the dried pasta. Cook until tender but firm. Drain in a colander.

5. Bring the sauce to a simmer. Add the drained pasta to the sauce and toss until all the ingredients are well combined. Serve immediately.

PLAN AHEAD

The entire sauce can be made 1 day in advance. Refrigerate.

*NOTE

You can substitute a small 7-ounce jar of drained roasted peppers for the yellow and red peppers.

If you haven't made up a batch of your own Tomato Sauce, you can use the commercially made brand of your choice.

For the Hot Sauce you can substitute 1/4 teaspoon Tabasco sauce.

Pasta with Spicy
Tomato Sauce and Prosciutto

2 tablespoons olive oil
2 tablespoons butter
2 cloves garlic, minced
1/4 cup minced shallots
1 small pickled hot pepper,
  minced*
1 cup Tomato Sauce*
6 tablespoons finely diced
  prosciutto

2 teaspoons salt
6 ounces dried linguini

1/4 cup grated Parmesan
  cheese

Serves 2–3

1. In a 10-inch sauté skillet, heat the olive oil and butter until the butter foams. Add the garlic and shallots; sauté over medium-low heat for about 2 minutes or until the garlic is lightly browned.

Add the pickled pepper; cook for a few seconds.

Add the tomato sauce and bring to a simmer.

Add the prosciutto and simmer another 30 seconds. Turn off the heat.

WHEN READY TO SERVE

2. Bring a large kettle of salted water to a rolling boil. Add the linguini. Cook until tender but firm. Drain in a colander.

3. Bring the sauce to a simmer. Add the drained linguini to the simmering sauce. With the heat on high, stir and toss 1 minute or until the sauce has been well combined with the pasta. Turn off the heat. Add the Parmesan cheese. Mix briefly and serve immediately.

PLAN AHEAD

If desired, the sauce can be prepared several days in advance.

*NOTE

Jars of pickled hot peppers can be found in most supermarkets.

If you haven't made up a batch of your own Tomato Sauce, you can use the commercially made brand of your choice.

Spaghetti with
Fresh Tomato Sauce and Basil

2 tablespoons olive oil
2 tablespoons butter
1/2 cup minced shallots
2 large garlic cloves, minced
4 cups diced very ripe fresh
  tomatoes
1 teaspoon salt
1 teaspoon sugar
Freshly ground black pepper
  (30 turns of the mill)

1/2 cup chopped fresh basil
  leaves*
1/4 cup chopped parsley

1 teaspoon salt
1/3 pound dried spaghetti

1/2 cup grated Parmesan
  cheese

Serves 2

1. In a 10-inch skillet, heat the olive oil and butter until the butter foams. Add the shallots and sauté 2 minutes over low heat. Add the garlic and sauté another minute or two, or until the shallots and garlic are lightly browned.

Add the tomatoes, salt, sugar, and pepper; simmer for about 30 minutes.

Add the basil and the parsley; simmer another minute.

WHEN READY TO SERVE

2. Bring a large kettle of salted water to a rolling boil. Add the spaghetti. Cook until tender but firm. Drain in a colander.

3. Bring the sauce to a simmer. Add the drained spaghetti to the simmering sauce. With the heat on high, stir and toss 1 minute or until the sauce has been well combined with the pasta. Turn off the heat. Add the Parmesan cheese. Mix briefly and serve immediately.

PLAN AHEAD

The sauce can be prepared 1 day in advance and refrigerated.

*NOTE

For the basil leaves you can substitute 1 tablespoon Pesto Base. Preferably use fresh Pesto Base rather than frozen.

Linguini with
Tomato and Sausages

2 tablespoons olive oil
1 cup chopped onions
1 1/2 tablespoons minced garlic
4 cups canned tomatoes with
   their juice*
1/4 cup Beef Stock
1 tablespoon Glace de
   Viande* (optional)
1/4 cup dry red wine
1/2 teaspoon salt
1/2 teaspoon sugar
1 tablespoon chopped parsley

1/4 pound sweet Italian
   sausage
1/4 pound hot Italian sausage
1 tablespoon sausage fat (see
   step 3)

2 teaspoons salt
1/2–2/3 pound dried linguini

1/2 cup grated Parmesan
   cheese

Serves 4–6

1. Preheat the oven to broil.

2. In a 12-inch sauté skillet, heat the olive oil over medium heat until it is hot. Add the onions and sauté over medium-low heat for about 2 minutes or until they are translucent.

Add the garlic and sauté another minute.

Add the canned tomatoes and their juice. Break them up while stirring. Add the beef stock and the glace de viande. Bring to a simmer over high heat; then turn the heat to medium.

Add the wine, salt, sugar, and parsley. Cook the sauce on medium heat at a fast simmer for 30 minutes.

3. While the sauce is simmering, prick the sausages with a poultry skewer in several places; then put them in a heatproof pan. Broil the sausages close to the heat source for about 10 minutes. Pour off the fat and discard. Prick the sausages again. Turn them over, then broil another 10 minutes. When the sausages are very well browned, remove them from the broiler. Reserve 1 tablespoon fat. Allow the sausages to cool, then slice them into 3/8-inch circles.

4. Add the 1 tablespoon sausage fat to the simmering sauce. Discard any remaining fat from the pan in which the sausages were broiled. Do not wash the pan.

5. Deglaze the pan in which the sausages were broiled with 1/2 cup of the simmering tomato sauce. Turn off the heat and add the contents of the pan to the skillet containing the tomato sauce.

Add the sliced sausages to the simmering sauce. Simmer another 5 minutes. Turn off the heat.

WHEN READY TO SERVE

6. Bring a large kettle of salted water to a rolling boil. Add the linguini. Cook until tender but firm. Drain in a colander.

7. Bring the sauce to a simmer. Add the linguini to the sauce. Turn the heat to high and toss until well combined. Turn off the heat. Add the Parmesan cheese. Toss well and serve immediately.

PLAN AHEAD

The entire sauce can be made a day in advance.

*NOTE

Four cups canned Italian tomatoes are contained in one 35-ounce tin.

You can make your own Glace de Viande or in some areas you can purchase it. It is also possible to make this dish successfully without it.

Fettucine with Tomato
Sauce and Crushed Nuts

1/4 cup pine nuts
1/4 cup walnuts
1 tablespoon olive oil
1 teaspoon minced garlic
2 tablespoons minced shallots
1 cup Tomato Sauce*
1/2 teaspoon salt
Freshly ground black pepper
(15 turns of the mill)
1 tablespoon Pesto Base*
1 tablespoon chopped parsley

2 teaspoons salt
1/2 pound fresh fettucine

1/4 cup grated Parmesan
cheese

GARNISH
Whole fresh basil leaves (when
available)

Serves 2–3

1. Preheat the oven to 325°. Place the pine nuts on an ungreased cookie sheet or an iron skillet and roast for 5 to 10 minutes or until they are golden brown. Allow to cool. Chop coarsely.

2. Chop the walnuts coarsely.

3. In a 10-inch skillet, heat the olive oil. Add the garlic and sauté about 30 seconds over low heat. Add the shallots and continue to sauté 2 minutes.

Add the tomato sauce. Bring to a simmer.

Add the salt and pepper; stir.

Add the pesto base, parsley, and nuts. Stir briefly, then turn off the heat.

WHEN READY TO SERVE

4. Bring a large kettle of salted water to a rolling boil. Add the fettucine and cook 2 to 3 minutes. Drain in a colander.

5. Bring the sauce to a simmer. Add the drained fettucine to the simmering sauce. With the heat on high, stir and toss 1 minute or until the sauce has been well combined with the pasta. Turn off the heat. Add the Parmesan cheese. Mix briefly and serve immediately. Garnish with fresh basil leaves.

*NOTE

If you haven't made up a batch of your own Tomato Sauce, you can use the commercially made brand of your choice.

Preferably use fresh Pesto Base rather than frozen.

Scampi with Pasta

Every time I eat scampi I sop up the sauce with tons of bread. Since
the sauce is as good as the shrimp, I decided I would try making
Scampi with Pasta.

1 pound medium-large shrimp (21–25 to the pound, or slightly bigger)	**1 tablespoon minced garlic**
	1/2 cup dry white wine
	1/4 cup bottled clam juice
	2 tablespoons chopped parsley
2 teaspoons salt	**1/2 teaspoon salt**
1/2 pound dried linguini	**Freshly ground black pepper (15 turns of the mill)**
4 tablespoons butter	**1/2 teaspoon dried oregano *or***
4 tablespoons olive oil	**1 teaspoon chopped fresh**
1/4 cup minced shallots	**oregano**

Serves 3–4

1. *To butterfly the shrimp:* Cut the shrimp along the convex side, but do
not let the knife go all the way through the meat. With the tip of the boning
knife, make a slit about 1 inch long in the middle of the shrimp on the
convex side. Push the tail of the shrimp through the slit. Pull the tail
through neatly.

2. Preheat the oven to broil. Start boiling water for pasta. Add the salt.
When the water comes to a rolling boil, add the linguini and boil until
tender but firm. Drain the pasta in a colander.

3. While the pasta is boiling, heat the butter and the oil in a heavy, oval-
shaped, heatproof dish with a lip over low heat until the butter foams.

Add the shallots and the garlic; and sauté 2 minutes.

Add the wine. Turn the heat to medium and simmer another minute.

Add the clam juice, parsley, 1/2 teaspoon salt, and pepper; simmer
another minute. Turn off the heat.

4. Dip each shrimp one at a time on both sides in the sauce. Line the
shrimp first around the lip of the pan, then continue filling in toward the
center. Sprinkle with oregano.

5. Broil the shrimp in the sauce for about 3 minutes or until they turn
pink.

6. Add the drained pasta to a heated serving dish. Pour the shrimp and
all the sauce over the pasta. Serve immediately.

Soup, Salad and Pasta Innovations
Pasta with Shrimp Fra Diavolo

Once I made this sauce with fresh Maine shrimp. An incredible culinary treat! Maine shrimp are tiny and pink before they are cooked. They are sold with their heads intact and are the sweetest shrimp I have ever tasted in my life. This wonderful variation on Lobster Fra Diavolo works beautifully, however, with any good-quality raw shrimp in the shell.

1/2 pound shrimp (small, 36–40 to the pound)	**1 teaspoon salt**
1 cup shrimp stock (see step 1)	**1 tablespoon chopped parsley**
2 tablespoons olive oil	**1/2 teaspoon dried oregano *or* 1 teaspoon chopped fresh oregano**
1/4 cup minced shallots	**1 teaspoon Hot Sauce***
1 teaspoon minced garlic	
1/2 cup dry white wine	**2 teaspoons salt**
3/4 cup Tomato Sauce*	**1/2 pound dried pasta**

Serves 2–3

1. Blanch the shrimp in 4 cups of water that have been brought to a rolling boil. The shrimp will cook in approximately 1 minute or less. When the shells turn pink, they are done. Remove the shrimp with a wire strainer or slotted spoon. Remove the shells. Deveining is not necessary. Leave whole. Add the shrimp shells to the water in which they were blanched and simmer uncovered 1 to 2 hours or until the stock has reduced to 1 cup. Strain the stock through a sieve lined with several layers of cheesecloth that have been rinsed and squeezed dry.

2. In a 10-inch sauté skillet, heat the oil until it is hot. Add the shallots and sauté over low heat for about 2 minutes or until they soften.

Add the garlic and continue to sauté for about 1 minute.

Add the white wine. Turn the heat to high and reduce by half.

Add the reserved shrimp stock and reduce by half.

Add the tomato sauce, salt, parsley, and oregano. Simmer over low heat for 2 minutes.

Add the Hot Sauce. Turn off the heat.

WHEN READY TO SERVE

3. Bring a large kettle of salted water to a rolling boil. Add the dried pasta and cook until tender but firm. Drain in a colander.

4. Bring the sauce to a simmer over high heat. Add the drained pasta to the sauce and toss to coat. Add the shrimp and toss again until the sauce and the pasta are well combined. Serve immediately.

PLAN AHEAD

   Pasta with Shrimp Fra Diavolo can be prepared several hours in advance
through step 2.

*NOTE

   If you haven't made up a batch of your own Tomato Sauce, you can use
the commercially made brand of your choice.

   For the Hot Sauce you can substitute 1/4 teaspoon Tabasco sauce.

Spaghetti with Puttanesca Sauce

I have substituted caviar for anchovies in my variation on Puttanesca Sauce, which is a Southern Italian sauce of garlic, tomatoes, capers, black olives, anchovies, and simple seasonings such as oregano and chili peppers. Translated it means sauce of the pleasure ladies. In Naples these ladies of the night like to come home and throw together a quick pasta, one in which the sauce takes about the same time as boiling the spaghetti. Besides being quick, this sauce is not expensive, even with the caviar, as the quality of the caviar is not crucial to the success of the dish.

2 teaspoons salt
1/3 pound dried spaghetti

3 tablespoons olive oil
2 cloves garlic, minced
1 cup Tomato Sauce*
**Freshly ground black pepper
  (5 turns of the mill)**

1/2 teaspoon Hot Sauce*
1/2 tablespoon Pesto Base*
**1/2 teaspoon chopped fresh
  oregano *or* 1/4 teaspoon
  dried oregano**
**1 tablespoon chopped pitted
  black olives***
1 ounce black caviar

Serves 2

1. Bring a large kettle of salted water to a rolling boil. Add the spaghetti. Cook until tender but firm. Drain in a colander.

2. While the spaghetti is boiling, heat the oil in a 10-inch skillet. Sauté the garlic over low heat for about 1 minute or until lightly browned.

Add the tomato sauce, pepper, and Hot Sauce. Heat until the tomato sauce simmers.

Add the pesto base, oregano, and black olives; stir briefly.

3. Add the drained spaghetti to the simmering sauce and toss until well combined. Turn off the heat. Gently stir in the caviar. Serve immediately.

*NOTE
If you haven't made up a batch of your own Tomato Sauce, you can use the commercially made brand of your choice.

For the Hot Sauce you can substitute 1/8 teaspoon Tabasco sauce.

Preferably use fresh Pesto Base rather than frozen.

If you have time to remove the pit, Niçoise olives are better than pitted black olives.

Linguini with Maraciara Sauce

Linguini with Maraciara Sauce is a Southern Italian dish. It is a variation on red clam sauce, but it has just a touch of tomato and lots of garlic. It is a perfect first course pasta that is not overly filling.

1 dozen fresh littleneck clams (very small) with their juice (see step 1)
4 tablespoons olive oil
2 tablespoons minced shallots
4 cloves garlic, minced
1/2 cup dry white wine
1/2 cup Tomato Sauce*

1 teaspoon Hot Sauce*
1/4 cup chopped parsley
1 teaspoon chopped fresh oregano *or* 1/2 teaspoon dried oregano

2 teaspoons salt
1/3 pound dried linguini

Serves 2

1. Have the fishmonger shuck the clams and place them in a container so all the juices are collected and saved. Remove the clams from the clam juice and dice. Line a sieve with a layer of cheesecloth that has been rinsed and squeezed dry. Pour the clam juice through the sieve and reserve.

2. In a 10-inch skillet, heat the olive oil. Add the shallots and garlic; sauté over low heat for about 3 minutes or until lightly browned.

Add the white wine; allow to reduce until it is evaporated by half.

Add the reserved clam juice, tomato sauce, Hot Sauce, parsley, and oregano; simmer a minute or two, or until the sauce blends and thickens somewhat. Turn off the heat.

WHEN READY TO SERVE

3. Bring a large kettle of salted water to a rolling boil. Add the linguini. Cook until tender but firm. Drain in a colander.

Bring the sauce to a simmer. Add the clams and simmer about 2 minutes. Add the drained linguini to the sauce. Stir and toss to coat well. Serve immediately.

PLAN AHEAD

Linguini with Maraciara Sauce can be prepared ahead several hours in advance through step 2. Refrigerate.

*NOTE

If you haven't made up a batch of your own Tomato Sauce, you can use the commercially made brand of your choice.

For the Hot Sauce you can substitute 1/4 teaspoon Tabasco sauce.

Fettucine Natasha

This dish combines two great delicacies, smoked salmon and caviar. It is my adaptation of an incredible and elaborate pasta dish that is from Pronto's, a restaurant in Toronto.

3 tablespoons butter
1/2 tablespoon olive oil
2 tablespoons minced shallots
1 clove garlic, minced
6 ounces smoked salmon, shredded
1/2 cup diced very ripe fresh tomatoes
Freshly ground black pepper (20 turns of the mill)
3 tablespoons vodka

1/2 cup heavy cream
2 tablespoons dry white wine
2 tablespoons Tomato Sauce*

2 teaspoons salt
3/4 pound fresh fettucine

GARNISH
2 tablespoons chopped parsley
1 tablespoon chopped dill
2 ounces black caviar

Serves 4–6

1. Bring a large kettle of water to a rolling boil.
2. While the water is coming to a boil, in a 12-inch sauté skillet heat 2 tablespoons of the butter and the olive oil until the butter foams.

Add the shallots and sauté over medium-low heat for about 2 minutes or until they have softened.

Add the garlic and sauté another minute.

Add the smoked salmon, tomatoes, and pepper. Allow to simmer while stirring for 2 minutes on high heat.

Add the vodka and allow it to reduce.

3. Turn the heat to low. Add the cream, white wine, and tomato sauce. Simmer another minute.

4. Add salt to the boiling water. Add the fettucine. Cook about 2 to 3 minutes. Drain in a colander.

Add the drained fettucine to the simmering sauce. With the heat on high, stir and toss 1 minute or until the sauce has been well combined with the pasta. Turn off the heat. Add 1 tablespoon butter. Stir and toss to coat well.

Portion out 4 to 6 servings. Garnish each serving with chopped parsley, dill, and caviar.

*NOTE
If you haven't made up a batch of your own Tomato Sauce, you can use the commercially made brand of your choice.

Capellini d'Angelo with Seafood

6 littleneck clams (very small)
1/4 pound shrimp, in the shell
1/4 pound scallops (bay or sea)
2 ounces red snapper fillet, skinned, *or* 2 ounces fresh salmon
2 tablespoons olive oil
3 tablespoons butter
1/4 cup minced shallots
2 tablespoons minced garlic
1/2 cup dry white wine

1 cup clam juice (combine bottled clam juice with natural clam juice from fresh clams)
1/4 cup chopped parsley
Freshly ground black pepper (10 turns of the mill)

2 teaspoons salt
1/2 pound dried capellini

Serves 2–4

1. Have the fishmonger shuck the clams and place them in a container so all the juices are collected and saved. Remove the clams from the clam juice and dice. Line a sieve with several layers of cheesecloth that have been rinsed and squeezed dry. Pour the clam juice through the sieve. Combine with bottled clam juice to make 1 cup. Reserve.

2. Shell, devein, wash, dry, and drain the shrimp; then dice.

3. Dice the scallops and red snapper. (If the bay scallops are very small, dicing is not necessary.)

4. Bring a large kettle of water to a rolling boil.

5. While the water is coming to a boil, in a 12-inch skillet heat the olive oil and 1 tablespoon of the butter until the butter foams. Add the shallots and garlic; sauté over low heat for about 2 minutes or until the garlic is lightly browned.

Add the white wine. Turn the heat to high and reduce by half.

Add the clam juice. Bring to a simmer and reduce by half over medium heat. This will take about 5 minutes.

6. Add the seafood, parsley, pepper, and the remaining 2 tablespoons of butter. Simmer 1 minute. Turn off the heat.

7. Add salt to the boiling water. Add the capellini. Cook until tender but firm. Drain in a colander. Add the drained capellini to the simmering sauce. With the heat on high, stir and toss 1 minute or until the sauce has been combined with the pasta. Turn off the heat. Serve immediately.

Angel's Hair with Lobster and Creamy Tomato Sauce

The only time-consuming part of the next three recipes is making the lobster stock, but it can simmer while you are puttering around the house. It is a crucial part, for the success of the sauce depends on the stock's intense flavor. This method calls for the lobster to be steamed whole, after which the meat is removed and the shells turned into a stock. All the lobster flavor is preserved. In any of these recipes, you can substitute 1/2 pound shrimp for the lobster. If using shrimp, blanch them for only 1 minute or until they turn pink. Remove the shells and return them to the stock, just as you would the lobster shells. As the stock is crucial to the seasoning of the sauce, raw shrimp with the shells must be used.

1 live 1 1/2-pound lobster	**Freshly ground black pepper**
1 cup lobster stock (see step 2)	**(10 turns of the mill)**
2 tablespoons butter	
2 tablespoons minced shallots	**2 teaspoons salt**
2 tablespoons chopped parsley	**1/2 pound fresh angel's hair**
2 tablespoons chopped dill	**pasta**
1 cup diced very ripe	
tomatoes	**1/3 cup heavy cream**
1/2 teaspoon salt	

Serves 2–3

1. In a stainless-steel or enamel 3-quart saucepan with a tight-fitting cover, bring 1 1/2 inches of water to a rolling boil. Put the lobster in the saucepan. Cover. Cook over high heat for about 1 minute or until the water starts to boil. Turn the heat to low and simmer the lobster for 7 minutes. Using tongs, remove the lobster from the saucepan and allow to drain and cool in a strainer with a bowl underneath. Leave the liquid in which it was boiled in the saucepan. When cool enough to handle, crack the shells and remove the lobster meat. Reserve any lobster juices that come out of the shell when you crack it. Dice the meat into 3/4-inch pieces. This will yield approximately 1 cup. If the lobster is female, add the roe and tomalley to the diced lobster meat. If male, add the tomalley.

2. Return the lobster shells, parts (with the exception of the brain, which should be discarded) and juices to the saucepan containing the reserved lobster liquid. Add 4 cups water. Bring to a boil over high heat, then turn the heat to low and simmer uncovered for about 1 1/4 hours or until the stock has reduced to 1 cup. Strain the stock through a sieve lined with 2 layers of cheesecloth that have been rinsed and squeezed dry. Reserve the lobster stock. Discard the shells.

WHEN READY TO SERVE

3. Bring a large kettle of water to a rolling boil.

4. While the water is coming to a boil, in a 10-inch skillet heat the butter until it foams. Add the minced shallots and sauté for about 2 minutes over low heat or until they have lightly browned.

Add the parsley and dill; continue to cook another few seconds.

Add the lobster stock, diced tomatoes, 1/2 teaspoon salt, and pepper. Turn the heat to high and reduce the lobster stock by half. This will take about 5 minutes.

5. Add salt to the boiling water. Add the pasta and cook 1 to 2 minutes. Drain in a colander.

6. Turn the heat to low and add the cream to the sauce. Stir well in a figure-8 motion to reach the center of the skillet. Add the pasta to the simmering sauce. Turn the heat to high and mix for about 1 minute. Add the diced lobster and continue to toss for another 30 seconds or until the lobster is heated through. Serve immediately.

PLAN AHEAD

Step 1 and step 2 can be done several hours in advance, in which case the lobster and stock should be refrigerated.

Spaghetti with
Red Lobster Sauce

What a delicious way to stretch a 1½-pound lobster into a dinner for four! It reminds me of the Chinese manner of doing things. One of my students, upon returning from a vacation in Italy, told me about a lobster sauce over pasta with tomato and basil. The idea appealed to me and resulted in this tasty creation.

1 live 1½-pound lobster	Freshly ground black pepper
1 cup lobster stock (see step 2)	(10 turns of the mill)
4 tablespoons olive oil	
½ cup minced shallots	2 teaspoons salt
6 cloves garlic, minced	⅔ pound dried spaghetti
1 cup dry white wine	
5 cups diced very ripe fresh	¼ cup chopped parsley
tomatoes *or* 1 cup Tomato	1 cup chopped basil leaves *or*
Sauce*	1 tablespoon Pesto Base*

Serves 3–4

1. In a stainless-steel or enamel 3-quart saucepan with a tight-fitting cover, bring 1½ inches of water to a rolling boil. Put the lobster in the saucepan. Cover. Cook over high heat for about 1 minute or until the water starts to boil. Turn the heat to low and simmer the lobster for 7 minutes. Using tongs, remove the lobster from the saucepan and allow to drain and cool in a strainer with a bowl underneath. Leave the liquid in which it was boiled in the saucepan. When cool enough to handle, crack the shells and remove the lobster meat. Reserve any lobster juices that come out of the shell when you crack it. Dice the meat small. This will yield approximately 1 cup. If the lobster is female, add the roe and tomalley to the diced lobster meat. If male, add the tomalley.

2. Return the lobster shells, parts (with the exception of the brain, which should be discarded), and juices to the saucepan containing the reserved lobster liquid. Add 4 cups of water. Bring to a boil over high heat, then turn the heat to low and simmer uncovered for about 1¼ hours or until the stock has reduced to 1 cup. Strain the stock through a sieve lined with 2 layers of cheesecloth that have been rinsed and squeezed dry. Reserve the lobster stock. Discard the shells.

3. In a 10-inch sauté skillet, heat the olive oil over medium heat. Add the shallots and garlic; sauté until they are lightly browned.

Add the white wine; allow the wine to boil until it has evaporated by half.

Add the diced tomatoes and pepper; simmer 20–30 minutes or until the sauce blends and thickens somewhat. If using tomato sauce, omit this simmering period.

WHEN READY TO SERVE

4. Bring a large kettle of salted water to a rolling boil. Add the pasta and cook until tender but firm. Drain in a colander.

5. Add the lobster stock to the sauce; simmer another 5 minutes or until the sauce has thickened.

Add the parsley and basil leaves; simmer another 1 minute.

Immediately add the drained pasta to the lobster sauce.

Add the diced lobster meat. With the heat on high stir and toss 1 minute or until the sauce has been well combined with the pasta. Serve immediately.

PLAN AHEAD

This sauce can be prepared early in the day through step 3, in which case refrigerate.

*NOTE

If you haven't made up a batch of your own Tomato Sauce, you can use the commercially made brand of your choice.

Preferably use fresh Pesto Base rather than frozen.

Soup, Salad and Pasta Innovations
Pasta with
Saffron, Lobster, and Fennel

Saffron has been mentioned in Italian cookbooks since the 1300s. It became especially popular in the Lombardy region of Northern Italy in the 1600s, when the Spanish dominated the Duchy of Milan. Before the advent of saffron, the Lombardy rich gilded their food. They started doing it not just because of the Renaissance emphasis on beauty but also because their alchemists told them that eating gold was good for their hearts. The alchemists' advice was gradually discarded, however, in favor of the golden appearance of the less expensive substitute. Even with the high cost of saffron today, Italians still add it to fresh pasta and risotto dishes.

1 live 1½-pound lobster	½ teaspoon salt
1 cup lobster stock (see step 2)	Freshly ground black pepper
2 grams saffron	(10 turns of the mill)
2 tablespoons butter	1 tablespoon Pernod
¼ cup minced shallots	
½ cup diced fennel	2 teaspoons salt
1 cup cherry tomatoes, cut in half	½ pound fresh pasta
2 tablespoons chopped parsley	1 tablespoon olive oil

Serves 2–3

1. In a stainless-steel or enamel 3-quart saucepan with a tight-fitting cover, bring 1½ inches of water to a rolling boil. Put the lobster in the saucepan. Cover. Cook over high heat for about 1 minute or until the water starts to boil. Turn the heat to low and simmer the lobster for 7 minutes. Using tongs, remove the lobster from the saucepan and allow to drain and cool in a strainer with a bowl underneath. Leave the liquid in which it was boiled in the saucepan. When cool enough to handle, crack the shells and remove the lobster meat. Reserve any lobster juices that come out of the shell when you crack it. Dice the meat into ¾-inch pieces. This will yield approximately 1 cup. If the lobster is female, add the roe and tomalley to the diced lobster meat. If male, add the tomalley.

2. Return the lobster shells, parts (with the exception of the brain, which should be discarded) and juices to the saucepan containing the reserved lobster liquid. Add 4 cups water. Bring to a boil over high heat, then turn the heat to low and simmer uncovered for about 1¼ hours or until the stock has reduced to 1 cup. Strain the stock through a sieve lined with 2 layers of cheesecloth that have been rinsed and squeezed dry. Discard the shells. While the lobster stock is still hot, add the 2 grams of saffron and allow to steep for 2 hours or longer.

3. In a 12-inch sauté skillet, heat the butter until it foams. Sauté the shallots over a medium heat for about 2 minutes or until they soften.

Add the fennel and continue to sauté for another 2 minutes.

Add the 1 cup lobster stock (do not strain the saffron from the stock) and reduce by half, still on a medium heat.

Add the tomatoes, parsley, ½ teaspoon salt, and pepper. Simmer 1 minute.

Add the Pernod and simmer another 2 minutes. Turn off the heat.

WHEN READY TO SERVE

4. Bring a large kettle of salted water to a rolling boil. Add the fresh pasta and cook 2 to 3 minutes. Drain in a colander.

Mix the pasta with 1 tablespoon of oil.

5. Add the pasta to the skillet containing the sauce. Turn the heat to high and mix the pasta with the sauce for about 1 minute or until the sauce begins to thicken.

Add the lobster meat and continue to toss until all the ingredients are well combined. Serve immediately.

PLAN AHEAD

Pasta with Saffron, Lobster, and Fennel can be prepared several hours in advance through step 3, in which case refrigerate.

Soup, Salad and Pasta Innovations
Mediterranean Pasta

I discovered this pasta creation at Café Max, a great restaurant in Pompano Beach, Florida. Mark Militello is their talented young chef. In my adapted version, I added olive paste, which gives the dish an interesting dimension of flavor. Olive paste has become a staple for me. I love to use it as a seasoning for pasta sauces and salads. It is sold in small glass jars and once opened should be stored in the refrigerator. If you top it with a little olive oil, it will last at least six months.

2 teaspoons salt	**1 tablespoon capers, rinsed**
1/3 pound dried capellini	**and drained**
	1 tablespoon olive paste
2 tablespoons olive oil	**2 tablespoons Niçoise olives**
3 tablespoons minced shallots	**2 tablespoons chopped parsley**
1 tablespoon minced garlic	**2 tablespoons vermouth**
1/2 teaspoon salt	**1/4 pound fresh tuna, skinned**
Freshly ground black pepper	**and cut in 1/8 × 1 × 1-inch**
(10 turns of the mill)	**pieces**

Serves 2–3

1. Bring a large kettle of salted water to a rolling boil. Add the capellini. Cook until tender but firm. Drain in a colander.

2. While the pasta is boiling, heat the olive oil in a 10-inch skillet until it is hot. Add the shallots and sauté over low heat for about 2 minutes. Add the garlic and continue to sauté another minute.

Turn the heat to medium and add the 1/2 teaspoon salt, pepper, capers, olive paste, olives, and parsley. Continue to stir until all the ingredients are well combined. Add the vermouth and tuna; stir one minute.

3. Add the drained pasta to the skillet. Toss until the pasta is coated. Serve at room temperature.

PLAN AHEAD

Mediterranean Pasta can be made several hours in advance and served at room temperature.

Fettucine with
Marsala and Porcini

This is a simple, speedy, and great-tasting pasta sauce that features sweet, nutty-flavored porcini, one of the finest-tasting mushrooms known to the world since the time of the ancient Greeks. As it is a rare event to find fresh porcini, it is fortunate that their flavor is captured and even intensified by drying them in the sun. Their large caps are cut into thin slices, dried, and packaged by the ounce. Try to find a store where they sell porcini by the pound. The price will be one quarter the amount. Split the cost with friends, give them as one-ounce treasures on special occasions, or store them one year in a wide-mouthed glass jar with a tight-fitting cover.

1 cup dried porcini
1 1/2 cups porcini liquid (see
   step 1)
3 tablespoons olive oil
1 tablespoon butter
1 tablespoon minced garlic
1 teaspoon salt
Freshly ground black pepper
   (10 turns of the mill)
1/2 cup dry marsala wine

2 teaspoons salt
1/2 pound fresh fettucine

1/4 cup grated Parmesan
   cheese

Serves 2–3

1. Place the porcini in a bowl and cover with 1 1/2 cups cold water. Soak 1/2 hour or until soft. Squeeze the porcini over the bowl, then shred. Line a sieve with 2 layers of cheesecloth that have been rinsed and squeezed dry. Pour the porcini liquid through the sieve; reserve 1 1/2 cups porcini liquid.

2. In a 10-inch skillet, heat the olive oil and butter until the butter foams. Add the garlic; sauté over low heat for about 1 minute or until lightly browned.

Add the porcini, salt, and pepper; sauté over medium heat for 2 minutes. Add the 1 1/2 cups porcini liquid. Simmer 7 to 8 minutes or until it has reduced by two thirds. Add the marsala wine, simmer 4 minutes or until reduced by half. Turn off the heat.

WHEN READY TO SERVE

3. Bring a large kettle of salted water to a rolling boil. Add the fettucine. Cook 2 to 3 minutes. Drain in a colander.

4. Bring the sauce to a simmer. Add the drained fettucine to the simmering sauce. With the heat on high, stir and toss 1 minute or until the sauce has been well combined with the fettucine. Turn off the heat. Add the Parmesan cheese. Mix briefly and serve immediately.

Pasta with
Asparagus and Porcini

1/2 cup dried porcini
3/4 cup porcini liquid (see
  step 1)
1 pound fresh asparagus

2 teaspoons salt
1/2 pound fresh pasta

1 tablespoon olive oil
3 tablespoons butter

3 tablespoons minced shallots
1/4 cup Chicken Stock
2 tablespoons chopped parsley
2 tablespoons vermouth
1 teaspoon salt
Freshly ground black pepper
  (10 turns of the mill)
1/4 cup heavy cream
1/2 cup grated Parmesan
  cheese

Serves 3–4

1. Place the porcini in a bowl and cover with 3/4 cup water. Soak 1/2 hour or until soft. Squeeze the porcini over the bowl, then shred. Line a sieve with two layers of cheesecloth that have been rinsed and squeezed dry. Pour the porcini liquid through the sieve; reserve 3/4 cup porcini liquid.

2. To determine the tender portion of the asparagus, hold the bottom of each stalk in the left hand in a gently closed fist. With the right hand, palm open, slap the green stalk so it breaks cleanly. Discard the tough portion. Then slant-cut each asparagus spear into 2-inch pieces. This should yield 2 cups.

3. To cook the pasta, bring a large kettle of salted water to a rolling boil.

4. While the water is coming to a boil, heat the oil and butter in a 10-inch skillet until the butter foams. Add the shallots and porcini. Sauté over medium heat for about 1 1/2 minutes.

Add the porcini liquid and chicken stock. Bring to a boil and reduce over medium-high heat by about 1/3. This will take about five minutes.

Add the asparagus, parsley, vermouth, salt, and pepper; simmer a few seconds. Turn the heat to low and then add the cream. Stir until blended. Turn off the heat.

5. Add the fresh pasta to the boiling water and cook 2 to 3 minutes. Drain in a colander.

6. Bring the sauce to a simmer over a low heat. Add the drained pasta. Stir and toss 1 minute or until the sauce has been combined with the pasta. Turn off the heat. Add the Parmesan cheese. Mix briefly and serve immediately.

Spaghetti with Porcini,
Pearl Onions, and Prosciutto

1/2 cup dried porcini
1 cup porcini liquid (see
   step 1)
1/2 cup pearl onions
1 tablespoon olive oil
1 tablespoon butter
1/2 cup shredded prosciutto
1/3 cup finely shredded red
   sweet peppers

1/4 cup heavy cream
2 tablespoons chopped parsley
Freshly ground black pepper
   (20 turns of the mill)

1 teaspoon salt
1/2 pound dried spaghetti

Serves 2–3

1. Place the porcini in a bowl and cover with 1 cup cold water. Soak 1/2 hour or until soft. Squeeze the porcini over the bowl, then shred. Line a sieve with 2 layers of cheesecloth which have been rinsed and squeezed dry. Pour the porcini liquid through the sieve and reserve.

2. Blanch the onions; then peel, leaving whole.

3. Bring a large kettle of water to a rolling boil.

4. While the water is coming to a boil, heat the oil and butter in a 10-inch skillet until the butter foams. Add the onions and sauté over the lowest possible heat for about 6 minutes or until they are almost cooked through.

Add the porcini liquid and reduce by half over medium-high heat.

Add the porcini; simmer another minute.

Add the prosciutto and sweet peppers; simmer 1 more minute.

5. Turn the heat to very low; add the cream, and simmer briefly. Add the parsley and pepper. Turn the heat off.

6. Add salt to the boiling water. Add the spaghetti. Cook until tender but firm. Drain in a colander. Add the spaghetti to the sauce. With the heat on high, stir and toss 1 minute or until the sauce has been well combined with the pasta. Turn off the heat. Serve immediately.

PLAN AHEAD

Although the cooking should be done just before serving, all the preparations can be done in advance.

Pasta with Wild Mushrooms

Sun-dried tomatoes have justifiably become a very popular Italian ingredient in America. I like to think of them as a seasoning, the way I do ginger in Oriental cooking. Sun-dried tomatoes have a stronger flavor than fresh tomatoes because when you dry any ingredient, it intensifies the flavor. The tomatoes are reconstituted in a seasoned olive oil. Stored on the shelf after opening, they will last several months, or in the refrigerator they will last over a year. I like to use them in salads (one or two diced in a salad gives the salad a nice spike). Or dice a few on top of open-faced sandwiches. Sometimes I can't wait till summer to have well-ripened tomatoes with slices of mozzarella, fresh basil, and a vinaigrette dressing on a bed of lettuce; so I substitute sun-dried tomatoes and my Pesto Base, which works beautifully.

1/2 cup dried porcini	**1/4 cup parsley**
1/4 cup porcini stock (see step 1)	**1/2 cup heavy cream**
	1 teaspoon salt
1/4 pound fresh chanterelles	**Freshly ground black pepper (20 turns of the mill)**
1/4 cup butter	
1 teaspoon minced garlic	
1/3 cup minced shallots	**2 teaspoons salt**
3 tablespoons sun-dried tomatoes*	**1/2 pound fresh pasta**

Serves 2–3

1. Place the porcini in a bowl and cover with 1 cup cold water. Soak 1/2 hour or until soft. Squeeze the porcini over the bowl, then shred. Line a sieve with 2 layers of cheesecloth that have been rinsed and squeezed dry. Pour the porcini liquid through the sieve; reserve 1 cup porcini liquid. Place the liquid in a saucepan and reduce over low heat until 1/4 cup remains. Reserve.

2. Rinse the chanterelles briefly under cold running water. Trim 1/2 inch from the stem, then shred.

3. Bring a large kettle of water to a rolling boil.

4. While the water is coming to a boil, in a 10-inch skillet heat the butter until it foams. Add the garlic and shallots; sauté over low heat for about 2 minutes or until lightly browned.

Add the porcini and chanterelles; sauté for about 2 minutes.

Add the porcini stock; reduce heat for 1 minute.

Add the sun-dried tomatoes, parsley, cream, salt, and pepper. Simmer a few minutes over the lowest possible heat. Turn off the heat.

5. Add salt to the boiling water. Add the pasta. Cook 2–3 minutes.

Drain in a colander. Bring the sauce to a simmer; add the drained pasta. Stir and toss to coat well. Turn off the heat. Serve immediately.

PLAN AHEAD

Although the cooking should be done just before serving, all the preparations can be done in advance.

*NOTE

The only drawback to sun-dried tomatoes is that they are expensive. A way of getting around this is to reconstitute them yourself, as sun-dried tomatoes that have not been reconstituted are only a fraction of the cost.

1. 1/4 pound sun-dried tomatoes (preferably from Italy, not California). Soak in warm water for 10 minutes. Drain.
2. Cover them with olive oil.
3. Mix in the following:

    1 tablespoon red wine vinegar

    1/2 teaspoon balsamic vinegar

    1 teaspoon dried basil
4. Place the whole mixture in a glass jar with a tight-fitting cover. They will be ready in one month.

Paglia e fieno
(Straw and Hay) with Sun-dried
Tomatoes and Porcini

In creating new dishes, I enjoy the elements of surprise and change. And when such a dish is a big success, it is a great source of satisfaction. When I was in Chicago recently, staying with cousins, I browsed through an inspiring shop called Convito's. Pastas are one of their specialities, including many of the condiments that help make great pasta sauces. My cousin said to me, "Would you make us a pasta tonight as part of our dinner?" First I chose the kind of pasta I wanted: paglia e fieno, which means straw and hay. Paglia e fieno is a mixture of yellow and green tagliatelle. The combination of the yellow egg noodles with the spinach noodles looks like straw and hay. In choosing ingredients to season the pasta, I kept in mind what the poet John Ciardi once said to me: "Words don't have to make sense, they should dance together." Here is the result.

3/4 cup dried porcini	**1 teaspoon salt**
1/4 cup porcini stock (see step 1)	**Freshly ground black pepper (10 turns of the mill)**
2 tablespoons olive oil	
1 tablespoon butter	**2 teaspoons salt**
1/4 cup minced shallots	**1/2 pound fresh tagliatelle**
1 tablespoon minced garlic	**1/2 pound fresh spinach tagliatelle**
1 tablespoon oil from sun-dried tomatoes	
3/4 cup shredded sun-dried tomatoes	**1 cup freshly grated Parmesan cheese**

Serves 4–6

1. Place the porcini in a bowl and cover with 1 1/2 cups cold water. Soak 30 minutes or until soft. Squeeze the porcini over the bowl, then shred. Line a sieve with 2 layers of cheesecloth that have been rinsed and squeezed dry. Pour the porcini liquid through the sieve. Place the liquid in a saucepan and reduce over low heat until 1/4 cup remains. Reserve.

2. Bring a large kettle of water to a rolling boil. While the water is coming to a boil, heat the olive oil and butter in a 12-inch skillet until the butter foams. Sauté the shallots and garlic in the skillet over low heat for about 2 to 3 minutes or until they are lightly browned.

Add the sun-dried-tomato oil and porcini; sauté another minute. Add the reduced and strained porcini stock; simmer a few seconds. Add the sun-dried tomatoes, the 1 teaspoon salt, and pepper. Stir briefly. Turn off heat.

3. Add salt to the boiling water. Add the pasta. Cook 2 to 3 minutes. Drain in a colander.

4. Bring the sauce to a simmer. Add the drained pasta to the simmering sauce. With the heat on high, stir and toss 1 minute or until the sauce has been well combined with the pasta. Turn off the heat. Add the Parmesan cheese. Mix briefly and serve immediately.

PLAN AHEAD

The sauce can be made several hours in advance.

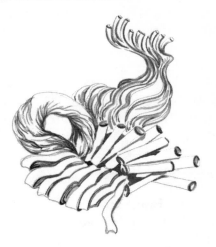

Soup, Salad and Pasta Innovations
Porcini Veal Sauce alla Parma

Parma, in the Emilia-Romagna region of Northern Italy, produces wonderful porcini mushrooms in the surrounding hills and the sweetest prosciutto in all of Italy. It is a natural evolution that a Parma chef would add these two ingredients to the classic Bolognese meat sauce from the neighboring city of Bologna.

Besides being excellent over fresh stuffed pastas such as tortellini and tortelloni, this sauce makes a wonderful lasagna. Try serving it over fresh green or egg noodles or homemade ravioli. It's so good I frequently serve it as an entree.

I have used the prosciutto as a seasoning, the way I use Smithfield ham in Chinese cooking. However, prosciutto is cured by being salted and air-dried, and is not smoked, like Smithfield ham and other Virginia and Kentucky hams. The salting, air-drying, and aging up to one year preserve it. It is often sliced paper-thin and served as an appetizer.

4 cups canned Italian tomatoes*	1 teaspoon salt
1/2 cup dried porcini	Freshly ground black pepper (20 turns of the mill)
1 cup porcini liquid (see step 2)	1 teaspoon sugar
4 tablespoons olive oil	1/2 cup finely diced prosciutto
2 tablespoons butter	1/2 cup chopped parsley
2 cups chopped onions	1/4 cup heavy cream
6 cloves garlic, minced	
1 pound coarsely ground shoulder of veal	2 teaspoons salt
	1 pound fresh stuffed pasta
1/2 cup dry white wine	
	1 cup grated Parmesan cheese

Serves 6–8

1. Pass the tomatoes through a food mill into a bowl. Reserve the puréed tomatoes with their juice; discard the seeds.

2. Place the porcini in a bowl and cover with 1 cup cold water. Soak 1/2 hour or until soft. Squeeze the porcini over the bowl. Set the porcini aside reserving the porcini liquid.

3. In a 12-inch sauté skillet, heat the olive oil and butter until the butter foams.

Add the onions and garlic; sauté over medium heat for about 3 to 4 minutes or until the onions and garlic have lightly browned.

Add the veal. Turn the heat to high, stirring constantly to crumble the veal. Cook for about 5 minutes or until the veal is white.

Add the wine and reduce heat for a few seconds.

Add the reserved tomatoes and juice to the sauté skillet. When the sauce begins to simmer, turn the heat to low and cook, stirring occasionally, for 30 to 40 minutes or until the sauce has been reduced by more than half.

4. Pour the porcini liquid into the sauce through a sieve lined with 2 layers of cheesecloth that have been washed and wrung dry. Chop the porcini and add them to the sauce.·

Add the 1 teaspoon salt, pepper, sugar, and prosciutto; simmer another 45 minutes or until the sauce is quite thick.

5. Add the parsley and cream; simmer a few more minutes. Turn off the heat.

WHEN READY TO SERVE

6. Bring a large kettle of salted water to a rolling boil. Add the stuffed pasta. Cook until tender but firm. Drain in a colander.

7. Bring the sauce to a simmer. Add the drained stuffed pasta to the simmering sauce. With the heat on high, stir and toss 1 minute or until the sauce has been well combined with the pasta. Serve with the Parmesan cheese.

PLAN AHEAD

This sauce can be made in advance through Step 5. It actually improves with age and will last five days in the refrigerator.

*NOTE

Four cups canned Italian tomatoes are contained in one 35-ounce tin.

Pasta with Chicken, Porcini, and Crème Fraîche

1 cup dried porcini
1½ cups porcini liquid (see step 1)
1 cup shallots
½ pound boneless skinless chicken breast
2 tablespoons olive oil
1 tablespoon butter
1½ teaspoons salt
Freshly ground black pepper (30 turns of the mill)

⅓ cup dry marsala wine
2 tablespoons chopped parsley
⅓ cup crème fraîche

2 teaspoons salt
½ pound fresh pasta, shaped like linguini

⅓ cup grated Parmesan cheese

Serves 2–3

1. Place the porcini in a bowl and cover with 1½ cups cold water. Soak ½ hour or until soft. Squeeze the porcini over the bowl, then shred. Line a sieve with 2 layers of cheesecloth that have been rinsed and squeezed dry. Pour the porcini liquid through the sieve and reserve. This will yield approximately 1½ cups.

2. Peel the shallots. In order to separate the shallots into their natural layer divisions, cut them in quarters lengthwise.

3. Remove all traces of fat and cartilage from the chicken breast. Then cut into small dice.

4. In a 10-inch skillet, heat the olive oil and butter until the butter foams. Add the shallots and sauté 2 minutes over low heat or until they begin to soften.

Add the porcini and continue to sauté another 2 minutes. Then add the 1½ teaspoons salt and pepper.

Turn the heat to high. Add all the porcini liquid and reduce for 3 minutes, or until reduced by half.

Add the marsala wine and cook 2 more minutes or until reduced by half.

Add the diced chicken and parsley; continue to cook another minute, stirring occasionally. Turn the heat to low.

Add the crème fraîche. Stir a few seconds, then turn off the heat.

WHEN READY TO SERVE
5. Bring a large kettle of salted water to a rolling boil. Add the fresh pasta and cook for about 2 or 3 minutes. Drain in a colander.

6. Bring the sauce to a simmer. Add the drained pasta to the simmering sauce. With the heat on high, stir and toss 1 minute or until the sauce has been well combined with the pasta. Turn off the heat. Add the Parmesan cheese. Mix briefly and serve immediately.

Spaghetti Carbonara

2 ounces sliced prosciutto
1/4 pound sliced bacon, cut crosswise into shreds
2 tablespoons bacon fat (see step 2)
1 tablespoon butter
1/2 cup chopped Spanish onions
1 teaspoon minced garlic
1/4 cup chopped parsley
1/2 cup heavy cream

2 teaspoons salt
10 ounces dried spaghetti

Freshly ground black pepper (10 turns of the mill)
1 egg, beaten (room temperature)
1/2 cup grated Parmesan cheese

Serves 4

1. Shred the prosciutto.

2. Bring a large kettle of water to a rolling boil. While the water is coming to a boil, fry the bacon shreds until crisp in a 10-inch skillet over medium-low heat. Remove the bacon from the skillet with a slotted spoon. Place the bacon in a colander set over a bowl and allow to drain. Pour all but 2 tablespoons of the bacon fat out of the skillet.

3. Add the butter to the skillet and sauté the onions over medium heat about 2 to 3 minutes or until soft. Add the garlic; sauté another 2 minutes or until the garlic is lightly browned. Turn the heat to low. Stir in the parsley, cream, and prosciutto. Cook about 2 to 3 minutes, stirring constantly. Remove from the heat.

4. Add salt to the boiling water. Add the spaghetti. Cook until tender but firm. Drain in a colander.

5. Return the sauce to a simmer, add the reserved bacon, and stir briefly. Place the drained spaghetti in the skillet containing the sauce. Toss well to coat. Turn off the heat. Add the pepper, the beaten egg and the cheese. Toss a few seconds and serve immediately.

Spaghetti with Bolognese Meat Sauce

This meat sauce is excellent over many different types of pasta, including spaghetti, spaghettini, linguini, tortellini, tortelloni, ravioli, or it can be used to make lasagna.

**4 cups canned Italian
tomatoes (measured with
their juice)***
2 tablespoons olive oil
2 tablespoons butter
1 cup chopped onions
2 cloves garlic, minced
1/4 cup chopped celery
**1/4 cup chopped carrot,
washed and scrubbed, but
not peeled**
**1 1/2 pounds ground lean beef,
preferably from the neck or
top of the rib**

2 teaspoons salt
2 cups dry white wine
1 cup milk
1/4 teaspoon nutmeg
**Freshly ground black pepper
(20 turns of the mill)**

2 teaspoons salt
1 pound dried spaghetti

Serves 6–8

1. Pass the tomatoes through a food mill into a bowl. Reserve the puréed tomatoes with their juice; discard the seeds.
2. In a 12-inch skillet, heat the oil and butter until the butter foams. Add the onions and garlic; sauté over medium heat for about 3 to 4 minutes or until the onions and garlic have lightly browned. Add the celery and carrot; sauté another two minutes. Add the ground beef and 2 teaspoons salt. Turn the heat to high, stirring constantly to crumble the beef. Cook for about 5 minutes or until the beef loses its red color.

Add the wine. Turn the heat to medium high and cook, stirring occasionally, until the wine has evaporated.

Turn the heat down to medium. Add the milk, nutmeg, and pepper; cook until the milk has evaporated. Stir frequently.

When the milk has evaporated, add the tomatoes and stir thoroughly. Return the sauce to a simmer over high heat. Turn the heat down and simmer uncovered for about 4 hours, stirring occasionally. Turn off the heat.

WHEN READY TO SERVE
3. Bring a large kettle of salted water to a rolling boil. Add the spaghetti. Cook until tender but firm. Drain in a colander.
4. Bring the sauce to a simmer. Add the drained spaghetti to the sim-

mering sauce. With the heat on high, stir and toss 1 minute or until the sauce has been well combined with the pasta.

PLAN AHEAD

This meat sauce can be made up to 5 days in advance, in which case refrigerate. It also freezes well for up to 2 months. Reheat until it simmers for about 15 minutes before serving.

*NOTE

Four cups canned Italian tomatoes are contained in one 35-ounce tin.

Lasagna Rolls Baked
with Meat Sauce

I love to make this dish for company. It is so unique to serve each
diner an individual roll or rolls of lasagna instead of cutting into a
casserole. This wonderful recipe was given to me by Carla Miner, one
of my students, who has had it in her family for years. The original
recipe called for cream cheese as one of the ingredients for the filling,
but I chose to update it with the addition of mascarpone, a fresh-milk
triple-cream Italian cheese that I use for spreading on bread, in pasta
sauces, and in desserts. The recipe is big, so cook it for a crowd. It is
also a lot of work, all of which can be done a day in advance. Just heat
it at the last moment.

MEAT SAUCE

**4 cups canned Italian
   tomatoes (measured with
   their juice)***

1 tablespoon olive oil

**3 sweet Italian sausages,
   casings removed, diced**

**1 1/2 pounds ground lean beef
   (top of the rib)**

1 tablespoon butter

2 cups chopped onions

1 teaspoon minced garlic

1/2 cup diced celery root*

2 tablespoons tomato paste

1 teaspoon sugar

1 teaspoon salt

1/4 cup chopped parsley

1 bay leaf

**1 teaspoon chopped fresh
   oregano *or* 1/2 teaspoon
   dried oregano**

**1/4 cup chopped fresh basil
   leaves *or* 1 tablespoon Pesto
   Base***

FILLING

4 tablespoons softened butter

1/2 pound mascarpone*

1/2 pound ricotta

**1/2 pound large-curd cottage
   cheese**

**1 tablespoon chopped
   scallions**

2 teaspoons chopped garlic

**1/2 cup grated Parmesan
   cheese**

1 teaspoon Dijon mustard

1/4 cup chopped parsley

3 egg yolks

**Freshly ground black pepper
   (20 turns of the mill)**

Butter for greasing pan

1 teaspoon salt

1 tablespoon olive oil

**1/2 pound lasagna, preferably
   fresh**

**1 pound mozzarella, thickly
   sliced**

Serves 12–16

1. *To prepare the meat sauce:* Pass the tomatoes through a food mill into a
bowl. Reserve the puréed tomatoes with their juice; discard the seeds.

2. In a 12-inch skillet, heat 1 tablespoon of olive oil over high heat until it is hot but not smoking. Add the sausages and the ground beef; break up the meat while cooking. Cook for 3 to 5 minutes or until the meats cook through. Empty the cooked meat into a colander set over a bowl. Allow to drain; shake the colander to aid the draining.

3. Do not wash the skillet; return it to medium heat. Add the 1 table-spoon butter. When it foams, add the onions; sauté 2 minutes or until they become translucent. Add the garlic; sauté another minute. Add the celery root; sauté one more minute. Add the puréed tomatoes with their juice, the drained meat, the tomato paste, the sugar, salt, parsley, bay leaf, and oregano. Simmer uncovered over the lowest possible heat for 3 hours or until the sauce is quite thick; stir occasionally. When the cooking is completed, add the basil. Remove the bay leaf.

4. *To prepare the filling:* Place the ingredients for the filling in a bowl and mix well with a wooden spoon.

5. Preheat the oven to 350°. Grease a 9 × 13-inch Pyrex baking dish with butter.

6. *To prepare the lasagna:* Bring a large kettle of salted water to a rolling boil. To prevent sticking, add 1 tablespoon of olive oil to the water. Add the lasagna. Keep separating the strips. If using dried lasagna, cook approximately 8 minutes (it should be slightly underdone). If using fresh lasagna, before boiling cut it into rectangular strips 2 inches wide by 4 inches long. Boil the fresh lasagna only about 1 to 2 minutes, depending on the thickness. Arrange the boiled lasagna over the sides of a colander and allow to drain. Place the lasagna in a bowl of cold water; separate and drain again. If using dried lasagna, cut the strips in half, crosswise.

7. Place approximately 2 tablespoons of the filling in the middle of a strip. Spread the filling evenly over the strip, leaving an inch at both edges; then roll it gently. Put the lasagna roll, seam end down, in the Pyrex dish. Roll the remaining strips, until all the filling is used. Arrange 3 rows of rolls. Do not layer. Spread the meat sauce over the lasagna. Cover with mozzarella slices.

8. Bake for 30 minutes. Once removed from the oven, let the lasagna rest for 10 minutes before serving. This will allow the filling to become more solid and will also enhance the flavor.

PLAN AHEAD

The entire preparation can be done a day in advance and refrigerated, in which case bring the lasagna to room temperature before baking.

*NOTE

Four cups canned Italian tomatoes are contained in one 35-ounce tin.

For the celery root you can substitute celery.

Preferably use fresh Pesto Base rather than frozen.

For the mascarpone you can substitute cream cheese.

Green Tagliolini with Veal Ragoût

A ragoût is a light stew of well-seasoned meat and vegetables cooked in a thick sauce. The word comes from *ragoûter,* which means "to stimulate the appetite." Ragoûts can be served three ways: as a stew, made into a soup by adding more stock, or tossed with pasta and made into a sauce. This fabulous sauce makes you feel as though you are having veal as your entree, but when you pay the grocery bill, you will feel as though you are adhering to a tight budget.

2 tablespoons corn oil
2 tablespoons olive oil
1 pound boneless veal, cut into 1/2-inch cubes*
1/4 cup diced shallots
1 cup chopped onions
1/4 cup diced carrots, scrubbed but not peeled
4 cloves garlic, crushed
2 anchovy fillets, diced
2 tablespoons chopped parsley
1 bay leaf
2 cups canned tomatoes, cut into pieces with their juice
1/2 cup white wine

1 1/2 cups Chicken Stock or Veal Stock
Freshly ground black pepper (20 turns of the mill)
1 teaspoon salt
1 tablespoon lemon juice
1 tablespoon tomato paste
1 tablespoon olive paste

2 teaspoons salt
2/3 pound fresh green tagliolini*

1/2 cup grated Parmesan cheese

Serves 4–6

1. In a 12-inch skillet, heat the corn oil and olive oil over high heat until it is hot but not smoking. Add half the veal and sauté 2 minutes or until the cubes have browned. Remove the veal from the skillet with a slotted spoon and add the remaining veal, stirring until the cubes have browned. Return the first portion to the skillet.

2. Add the shallots and stir for a minute. Then add the onions and carrots and sauté for another 2 minutes.

Add the garlic and anchovy fillets and stir for a few seconds.

Add the parsley, bay leaf, tomatoes with their juice, white wine, 1 cup of the stock, the pepper, 1 teaspoon salt, lemon juice, and tomato paste. Stir well. Bring to a simmer over high heat. Turn the heat to low. Cover and simmer 1 hour, checking every 20 minutes or so to see that the sauce is not evaporating too quickly.

3. After 1 hour, if the sauce is too thick, add 1/2 cup of chicken or veal stock. Simmer the sauce another 1/2 hour or until the veal is very tender and the sauce has thickened. If the veal becomes soft before the sauce has

thickened, remove the cover and reduce the sauce until the right consistency is obtained.

Stir in the olive paste. Turn off the heat. Remove the bay leaf.

WHEN READY TO SERVE

4. Bring a large kettle of salted water to a rolling boil. Add the tagliolini and cook 2 to 3 minutes. Drain in a colander.

5. Bring the veal ragoût to a simmer. Add the drained tagliolini to the sauce. Stir well to coat. Turn off the heat. Add the Parmesan cheese. Toss well and serve immediately.

PLAN AHEAD

Veal Ragoût can be made several days in advance, and refrigerated. It also freezes well.

*NOTE

There are several choices for cuts of veal that you can use. My first choice is second-cut sirloin of veal, which is the lower portion of a boneless rack of veal. If all this sounds too complicated, just ask your butcher for a boneless piece of veal, whether it be shoulder or neck, that contains no gristle and that is suitable for braising.

For the tagliolini, you can substitute other fresh pastas such as tagliatelle or fettucine.

Duck Ragoût with Bow-tie Pasta

You don't often run into a great Italian chef and restaurateur who is willing to share her secrets with you. Lidia Bastianich of Felidia's in New York City is one of those rare people. She came to my cooking school and showed me and my students how to make this wonderful Duck Ragoût, which is a Northern Italian dish. Although this sauce is not a speedy one, it can be made a day in advance, just like a stew.

1/2 **cup porcini**
1 **cup porcini liquid (see**
   step 1)
2 **whole ducks***
2 **tablespoons olive oil**
1/4 **cup corn oil**
Salt to taste
Freshly ground black pepper
   (30 turns of the mill)
2 **slices bacon, diced***
1 **cup chopped Spanish onions**
1/2 **cup chopped shallots**
1/2 **cup diced chicken livers**

4 **bay leaves**
1 **whole stem fresh rosemary**
   or 1/2 **teaspoon dried**
   rosemary
6 **cloves**
2 **tablespoons tomato paste**
3/4 **cup dry white wine**
4 **cups Chicken Stock**

2 **teaspoons salt**
1 **pound dried or fresh bow-**
   tie pasta

1 **cup grated Parmesan cheese**

Serves 6–8

1. Place the porcini in a bowl and cover with 1 cup cold water. Soak 1/2 hour or until soft. Squeeze the porcini over the bowl, then dice. Line a sieve with 2 layers of cheesecloth that have been rinsed and squeezed dry. Pour the porcini liquid through the sieve and reserve.

2. *To bone the ducks:* Remove the legs and wings by cutting through the separation at the joint. Remove the tail and discard. Remove and discard the skin from every part of the duck except the wings. Remove the meat from the breast, thighs, and legs. Trim away any fat from the meat. Reserve the carcass, including the leg and neck bones, and the wings. Dice the meat into 3/4-inch cubes. Set aside.

3. Heat the olive oil and corn oil in a 12 to 14-inch skillet with high sides or a 5-quart casserole. Add 1/4 of the boned duck meat, stirring over high heat until it turns a reddish brown. With a slotted spoon, remove the duck meat and add the next quarter. Repeat the same process until all the duck meat has been browned.

4. Return the seared duck meat to the skillet. Add the salt and pepper.

Stir a minute or two. Over medium heat, add the duck necks and bacon. Sauté a few minutes. Add the onions and sauté a few minutes. Add the shallots and sauté another few minutes. Then add the chicken livers, porcini, bay leaves, rosemary, and cloves. Stir a few seconds. Add the tomato paste; stir a few seconds. Add the porcini liquid, wine, and chicken stock, along with the reserved carcass, including legs and wings. Bring to a boil. Cover and simmer for 45 minutes. Remove cover, turn heat to low, and let the sauce reduce, simmering for another 15 minutes or so.

5. Remove all the bones and discard. Reduce the sauce, uncovered, over medium-low heat for about 1 more hour or until the sauce is quite thick. Remove the bay leaves, cloves, and rosemary stem.

WHEN READY TO SERVE

6. Bring a large kettle of salted water to a rolling boil. Add the pasta. Cook until tender but firm. Drain in a colander.

Bring the sauce to a simmer. Add the drained pasta to the simmering sauce. With the heat on high, stir and toss 1 minute or until the sauce has been well combined with the pasta. Turn off the heat. Add the Parmesan cheese. Mix briefly and serve immediately.

PLAN AHEAD

Duck Ragoût can be made ahead through Step 5 up to two days in advance. Refrigerate.

*NOTE

If boning a duck seems too awesome, you can substitute 1½ pounds of diced shoulder of veal or 1½ pounds of diced skinless, boneless chicken.

For the bacon, you can substitute 1 slice diced pancetta.

Fettucine Alfredo with Mascarpone

Mascarpone is a fresh-milk triple-cream Italian cheese. I would say it is Italy's answer to crème fraîche. The consistency of mascarpone is more like our American cream cheese, only softer. As it lasts no longer than a quart of milk, always ask to taste it before you buy it. After a few days it develops a slight aftertaste, like the nutty flavor of crème fraîche, but once it has soured it can no longer be used.

3 tablespoons butter
3/4 cup mascarpone at room temperature
2 tablespoons heavy cream
1/2 teaspoon salt
Freshly ground black pepper (20 turns of the mill)

1 teaspoon salt
2/3 pound fresh fettucine

1/2 cup grated Parmesan cheese
1 pinch nutmeg

Serves 3–5

1. In a 10-inch skillet, melt the butter over low heat. Add the mascarpone and cream; slowly stir until smooth. Add the 1/2 teaspoon salt and the pepper. Turn off the heat.

2. Bring a large kettle of salted water to a rolling boil. Add the fettucine. Cook about 2 to 3 minutes. Drain in a colander.

3. Bring the sauce to a simmer over low heat. Add the drained fettucine. Stir and toss 1 minute or until the sauce has been well combined with the pasta. Turn off the heat. Add the Parmesan cheese and nutmeg. Mix briefly and serve immediately.

Fettucine Cantilena

Fettucine Cantilena is like a smooth, flowing melodic phrase. It features two celebrated cow's-milk cheeses from the Lombardy region of Italy. Gorgonzola, which is the name of a village in Northern Italy near Milan, is the foremost blue-veined Italian cheese. It is a cured cheese, creamy in texture and sharp in flavor. It contrasts beautifully with the more lyrical mascarpone—a soft, rich, fresh-milk cheese with a mild, buttery flavor.

4 ounces mascarpone
4 ounces Gorgonzola
2 tablespoons butter
1 cup diced Spanish onions
1 cup Chicken Stock
1/2 cup shredded prosciutto
1/4 cup chives, cut in 1/8-inch rounds

2 tablespoons chopped parsley
Freshly ground black pepper (15 turns of the mill)

2 teaspoons salt
3/4 pound fresh fettucine

Serves 4–6

1. Bring the mascarpone and Gorgonzola to room temperature. Combine the cheeses in a bowl with a fork.

2. In a 10-inch skillet, heat the butter until it foams. Add the onions and sauté over low heat for about 6 minutes or until dark brown and nicely caramelized. Drain the remaining butter. Add the chicken stock and reduce by half over medium-high heat. Turn the heat to low. Add the combined cheeses. Stir until well blended. Add the prosciutto, chives, parsley, and pepper. Stir briefly. Turn off the heat.

WHEN READY TO SERVE

3. Bring a kettle of salted water to a rolling boil. Add the fettucine. Cook two or three minutes. Drain in a colander.

4. Bring the sauce to a simmer. Add the drained fettucine. Stir and toss until well combined. Turn off the heat. Serve immediately.

Linguini with Pesto Genoese

During the time of the First Crusades, one soldier on his way to the Holy Land wrote that "every evening, at dinner time, from a certain part of the camp came a fragrance of garlic and basil. That part of the camp was the Genoese quarters, easily recognizable, simply with the help of the nose." My variation on this popular classic still has fresh summer basil as its star ingredient. The addition of broiled mushrooms and sautéed shallots adds another flavorful dimension. Since the featured ingredient of the sauce is basil, it is best to use fresh summer basil when it is at its peak.

2 tablespoons pine nuts	**Freshly ground black pepper**
1 cup fresh mushrooms,	**(10 turns of the mill)**
washed and sliced	1/2 cup Pesto Base
3 tablespoons Chicken Stock	
1 tablespoon olive oil	2 teaspoons salt
1 tablespoon butter	1/2 pound dried linguini
1 clove garlic, minced	
2 tablespoons minced shallots	1/2 cup grated Parmesan
1 teaspoon salt	cheese

Serves 2–3

1. Preheat the oven to 325 degrees. Roast the pine nuts on a cookie sheet or in an iron skillet for 5 to 10 minutes or until they are golden brown. Remove them from the oven; reserve.

2. Turn the oven to broil. Allow 10 minutes for the temperature to rise. Broil the mushrooms in an iron skillet for about 6 minutes. Remove from oven. Place the skillet over a low heat; pour the chicken stock into the skillet and allow to reduce to 1 tablespoon stock.

3. Bring a large kettle of water to a rolling boil. While the water is coming to a boil, heat the olive oil and butter in a 10-inch skillet until the butter foams. Add the garlic and shallots; sauté over low heat for about 2 minutes or until lightly browned.

Add the mushrooms and the stock (from the iron skillet), along with the 1 teaspoon salt, pepper, and pesto base; stir until well combined. Turn off the heat.

4. Add salt to the boiling water. Add the linguini. Cook until tender but firm. Drain in a colander.

5. Bring the sauce to a simmer. Add the drained pasta to the sauce. Simmering with the heat on high, stir and toss 1 minute or until the sauce has been well combined with the pasta.

Add the nuts. Mix well.

Turn off the heat. Add the Parmesan cheese. Mix briefly and serve immediately.

Linguini with Broccoli de Rape

If you go to an Italian restaurant in the fall when broccoli de rape is at its best, you won't find this simple pasta dish listed on the menu but it will be on every plate.

2 pounds fresh Italian broccoli de rape

3/4 pound dried linguini
2 teaspoons salt

1/3 cup olive oil
3 tablespoons minced garlic

1 1/4 cups Chicken Stock
Salt to taste
Freshly ground black pepper (30 turns of the mill)

1/2 cup grated Parmesan cheese

Serves 4–6

1. Wash, drain, then dry the broccoli. Trim the broccoli, discarding at least 3 to 4 inches of the stem. Cut the remaining portion in half (about 3-inch lengths). This will yield approximately 1 1/4 pounds of the trimmed broccoli.

2. Bring 1 gallon of water to a rolling boil. Blanch the broccoli 1 minute. After the broccoli is blanched, set it over a colander to drain.

3. Cook the linguini in the boiling water in which the broccoli was blanched, adding 2 teaspoons of salt to the water. Cook until tender but firm. Drain in a colander. Set aside.

4. Heat the olive oil in a sauté skillet. Add the garlic. Sauté until the garlic turns slightly golden.

Add the chicken stock. Bring to a rapid boil; reduce for 2 minutes.

Add the broccoli. Toss the broccoli over high heat for 1 minute.

Add the salt, pepper and the linguini to the sauté skillet and mix well. Turn off the heat and add the Parmesan cheese. Toss briefly. Serve in individual pasta bowls.

PLAN AHEAD
   Although the cooking should be done just before serving, all the preparations can be done in advance.

Soup, Salad and Pasta Innovations
Spaghettini Mezzanotte

A much beloved, rather Bohemian dish that the sophisticates of Rome adopted long ago is an unpretentious pasta of garlic and oil called Aglio e Olio. Spaghettini Mezzanotte is similar to Aglio e Olio in its ease, simplicity, and taste. The Parmesan cheese, onions, and shallots make it somewhat heartier. It also differs in that the seasonings are slightly more elaborate. The most important ingredient, however, is shared: both require a superior-quality olive oil, whose full, fruity, rich, complex taste is crucial to the flavor of the dish.

   A good bottle of olive oil, like a good bottle of wine, is a matter of personal preference. There are fine Tuscan oils, fruity Sicilian oils, "extra virgin," "virgin," and "pure" olive oils. Those in the "pure" category can be used in other dishes, but ideally not in this one. "Pure" olive oil is from the second pressing of the olives or a mixture of first and second pressings. This refined oil with its light color has a flavor that lacks the character of "virgin" and "extra virgin" olive oils. Both "virgin" and "extra virgin" olive oils come from the first pressing of the olives and are unrefined. "Virgin" uses a lower grade of olive. The dark green oil of high-quality olives, which are often pressed by hand, is labeled "extra virgin." It tastes, looks, and smells like green olives. It becomes even more precious when you think of the olives being picked by hand or combed out of the trees with wooden-toothed rakes. To obtain fifteen pounds of oil requires gathering one hundred pounds of olives. Fine olive oil is a tradition in the Mediterranean region, as the olive has been cultivated there since 3000 B.C.

2 teaspoons salt	**Freshly ground black pepper**
1/2 pound dried spaghettini	**(20 turns of the mill)**
	2 tablespoons parsley
1/4 cup olive oil	
1 tablespoon sliced garlic	**1/4 cup Parmesan cheese**
1/4 cup chopped onions	**1 tablespoon oil from sun-**
1/4 cup minced shallots	**dried tomatoes***
1/2 teaspoon salt	

Serves 2–3

1. Bring a large kettle of salted water to a rolling boil. Add the spaghettini. Cook until tender but firm. Drain in a colander.
2. In a 10-inch skillet, heat the olive oil. Add the garlic and sauté over low heat about 30 seconds. Add the onions and continue to sauté about 2 minutes. Add the shallots and sauté another minute. Add the 1/2 teaspoon salt, pepper, and parsley.

3. Add the drained spaghettini to the skillet. Toss to coat. Turn off the heat. Add the Parmesan cheese. Mix briefly. Add 1 tablespoon oil from sun-dried tomatoes and toss again. Serve immediately.

*NOTE

Olive oil can be substituted for the sun-dried-tomato oil.

Pasta with Peas and Shallots

2 teaspoons salt
1/2 pound dried pasta

1 1/2 tablespoons olive oil
1 1/2 tablespoons butter
1/3 cup minced shallots
2/3 cup red sweet pepper, cut
  into small triangles
1 1/2 pounds fresh unshelled
  peas *or* 1 1/2 cups shelled
  peas*

2 tablespoons chopped parsley
1/4 cup Chicken Stock
2 tablespoons dry white wine
Salt to taste
Freshly ground black pepper
  (20 turns of the mill)
1 tablespoon crème fraîche*
1/4 cup Parmesan cheese

Serves 3–4

1. Bring a large kettle of salted water to a rolling boil. Add the pasta. Cook until tender but firm. Drain in a colander.

2. In a 10-inch skillet, heat the olive oil and butter until the butter foams. Add the shallots; sauté over low heat for about 3 minutes or until they soften.

3. Turn the heat to medium. Add the red sweet peppers. Sauté another minute. Add the peas, parsley, chicken stock, wine, salt, and pepper. Cook the fresh peas over medium-low heat for about 5 minutes. If using frozen peas, cook about 2 minutes.

Add the crème fraîche; toss briefly.

4. Add the drained pasta to the simmering sauce. With the heat on high, stir and toss 1 minute or until the sauce has been combined with the pasta. Add the Parmesan cheese. Mix briefly and serve immediately.

*NOTE
Frozen peas can be substituted for the fresh peas, in which case you should defrost them.

For the crème fraîche an equal amount of heavy cream can be substituted.

Pasta with Spring Vegetables
and Crème Fraîche

Sometimes I get ideas for recipes from a person who describes a dish to me, even though I have never tasted it. A student, back from a vacation in France, raved about a vegetable dish in which the carrots and zucchini were cut into the thinnest of julienne pieces and slowly sautéed in butter. From this description I invented the following recipe, which I enriched with crème fraîche and freshly grated Parmigiano-Reggiano (Parmesan) Cheese.

1 teaspoon salt	Freshly ground black pepper
1/2 pound dried pasta	(20 turns of the mill)
	4 cups shredded, unpeeled
3 tablespoons olive oil	zucchini
3 tablespoons butter	1/2 cup crème fraîche*
1/2 cup minced shallots	6 tablespoons Pesto Base*
2 cloves garlic, minced	1/2 cup chopped parsley
1 1/2 cups shredded carrots,	
washed and scrubbed, but	1 cup freshly grated Parmesan
not peeled	cheese
2 teaspoons salt	

Serves 2–3

1. Bring a large kettle of salted water to a rolling boil. Add the pasta. Cook until tender but firm. Drain in a colander.

2. In a 12-inch skillet heat the oil and butter over medium-low heat until the butter foams. Add the shallots, garlic, and carrots. Sauté about 2 to 3 minutes or until the garlic is lightly browned. Add the 2 teaspoons salt and pepper.

Turn the heat to high. Add the zucchini and sauté another minute or until the zucchini has cooked almost all the way through but is still crisp.

Turn the heat to low. Add the crème fraîche, pesto base, and parsley. Stir well.

3. Add the drained pasta to the simmering sauce. With the heat on high, stir and toss 1 minute or until the sauce has been well combined with the pasta. Turn off the heat. Add the Parmesan cheese. Mix briefly and serve immediately.

*NOTE

For the crème fraîche an equal amount of heavy cream can be substituted.

Preferably use fresh Pesto Base rather than frozen.

Orzo Primavera

Orzo, which is a dried pasta in the shape of rice, invites you to be creative. Orzo Primavera is a very versatile side dish in that it is equally good hot or at room temperature and it goes well with many different main courses, such as roast chicken or broiled fish. One of my favorite ways to serve it is as an accompaniment to sautéed veal chops. Although I created Orzo Primavera as a pasta dish, it is excellent with both Italian and American fare.

2 teaspoons salt	**1 cup diced unpeeled zucchini**
1/2 pound dried orzo	**1/4 cup Chicken Stock**
	1/4 cup Tomato Sauce
1/4 cup olive oil	**1 cup frozen peas (defrosted)**
1 cup diced red sweet peppers	**Salt to taste**
2/3 cup diced yellow Holland peppers	**Freshly ground black pepper (10 turns of the mill)**
2 tablespoons minced shallots	**1/2 cup grated Parmesan cheese**
1 tablespoon minced garlic	
1/4 cup carrots, cut in circles	
1/2 cup string beans, cut in circles	

Serves 8–10

1. Bring a large kettle of salted water to a rolling boil. Add the orzo. Cook about 4 minutes or until tender but firm. The orzo should be slightly underdone. Drain in a colander.

2. In a 10-inch skillet, heat the olive oil. Add the red and yellow peppers; sauté 10 minutes over very low heat.

Add the shallots and sauté 1 minute over a medium heat.

Add the garlic and sauté another minute.

Add the carrots and string beans; sauté 2 minutes.

Add the zucchini and mix briefly.

Add the stock and bring to a simmer.

Add the tomato sauce, peas, salt, and pepper. Stir until well combined.

3. Add the drained orzo; turn the heat to high and stir until all the sauce is absorbed into the orzo.

Turn off the heat; add the Parmesan cheese. Mix briefly. Empty the contents into a serving bowl. Serve hot or at room temperature.

PLAN AHEAD

Orzo Primavera can be made several days in advance and refrigerated. Bring to room temperature before serving.

Spaghetti with Salsa Forte

It started with a cup of leftover Eggplant in Garlic Sauce, which is like a Chinese version of ratatouille. Pasta sauces were on my mind and the idea of combining a Chinese and an Italian sauce appealed to me. I naturally had some of my homemade basic Tomato Sauce on hand, since I keep it in stock as I do mustard or a quart of milk. Then the recipe expanded with the addition of sun-dried tomatoes, olive paste, and mascarpone, which also have become staples to me. Now Salsa Forte is one of my favorite sauces, as it is spicy, original, and speedy, providing you have on hand the basic Tomato Sauce and the Eggplant in Garlic Sauce.

1 cup Eggplant in Garlic Sauce*

2 cups Tomato Sauce*

1/4 cup diced sun-dried tomatoes

1/4 cup mascarpone*

2 tablespoons chopped parsley

2 teaspoons salt

1/2 pound dried spaghetti

Serves 2–4

1. Dice the Eggplant in Garlic Sauce into smaller pieces.
2. In a 10-inch skillet, bring the tomato sauce to a simmer over a low heat.

Add the Eggplant in Garlic Sauce and simmer a minute, stirring occasionally.

Add the sun-dried tomatoes; simmer another 2 minutes, stirring occasionally.

Add the mascarpone and parsley; simmer 1 more minute. Turn off heat.

WHEN READY TO SERVE

3. Bring a large kettle of salted water to a rolling boil. Add the spaghetti. Cook until tender but firm. Drain in a colander.
4. Bring the sauce to a simmer. Add the drained pasta to the simmering sauce. With the heat on high, stir and toss 1 minute or until the sauce has been well combined with the pasta. Turn off the heat. Serve immediately.

*NOTE

For the Eggplant in Garlic Sauce, you can substitute ratatouille or Spicy Pepper Salad.

If you haven't made up a batch of your own Tomato Sauce, you can use the commercially made brand of your choice.

Mascarpone is a fresh-milk Italian cheese. If necessary, you can substitute crème fraîche or heavy cream.

Soup, Salad and Pasta Innovations
Linguini with Neapolitan Sauce

This is a superior sauce of vegetables, hearty with its eggplant and zucchini and exuberant with its olive-scented tomato base. The idea for this particular sauce came about as an offshoot of Salsa Forte. What if you were in the mood for a pasta featuring eggplant, as Salsa Forte does, but didn't have any leftover Eggplant in Garlic Sauce (a crucial ingredient) and couldn't find a good-quality prepared ratatouille as its substitute? Neapolitan Sauce is the answer, and it has become as popular with students as Salsa Forte. They constantly discover new ways to use it. Besides pasta, they use it as a topping for pizza and for melted-cheese sandwiches. I frequently serve it also as a condiment for hamburger and as an accompaniment to roast chicken.

4 cups canned Italian tomatoes (measured with their juice)*
3 tablespoons olive oil
3 tablespoons butter
6 cloves garlic, minced
1 1/4 cups chopped onions
1 cup finely diced unpeeled eggplant
1 cup finely diced unpeeled zucchini
1/2 cup diced red sweet pepper
1 tablespoon olive paste*

1/4 cup diced sun-dried tomatoes
2 tablespoons chopped parsley
1 tablespoon oil from sun-dried tomatoes
1 teaspoon salt
1 teaspoon sugar
2 teaspoons Hot Sauce*
1/4 cup mascarpone*
1/4 cup Pesto Base*

2 teaspoons salt
3/4 pound dried linguini

Serves 6–8

1. Pass the tomatoes through a food mill into a bowl. Reserve the puréed tomatoes with their juice; discard the seeds.

2. In a 12 to 14-inch skillet, heat the olive oil and butter until the butter foams. Add the garlic and onions; sauté over medium heat for about 3 minutes or until lightly browned.

Add the puréed tomatoes and simmer uncovered 10 minutes.

Add the eggplant and simmer uncovered about 20 minutes.

Add the zucchini and the red pepper; simmer uncovered another 10 minutes.

Add the remaining sauce ingredients and simmer uncovered 2 minutes. Turn off the heat.

WHEN READY TO SERVE

3. Bring a large kettle of salted water to a rolling boil. Add the linguini. Cook until tender but firm. Drain in a colander.

4. Bring the sauce to a simmer; add the drained linguini. Stir and toss to coat well. Turn off the heat. Serve immediately.

PLAN AHEAD

Neapolitan Sauce improves with age and is best made at least one day in advance. It will keep for up to 5 days, or can be frozen for up to 2 months.

*NOTE

Four cups canned Italian tomatoes are contained in one 35-ounce tin.

For the olive paste, you can substitute ¼ cup shaved olives, the first choice of olive being Niçoise.

For the Hot Sauce you can substitute ½ teaspoon Tabasco sauce.

For the mascarpone, you can substitute an equal amount of crème fraîche or heavy cream.

Preferably use fresh Pesto Base rather than frozen.

Penne Rigate with
Red-cooked Shoulder of Pork

Red-cook simmering is an ancient Chinese cooking technique that is similar to braising. Whole pieces of meat, fish, or poultry are slowly simmered for a long time until very tender. The simmering liquid always contains a generous quantity of soy sauce, giving the meat a very slight reddish cast. Red rice is sometimes added to give a further reddish effect. The outcome is actually more dark brown than red, but because of the Chinese preference for the color red, they call the technique red-cook simmering.

   Always a winter favorite, Red-cooked Shoulder of Pork is an old standby for me. Recently I tried this savory stew over pasta with great success.

1 medium leek	**2 slices ginger**
1 fresh shoulder of pork, 3–4 pounds*	**3 cups salt-free Chicken Stock***
1/4 cup Chinese mushrooms	**2 tablespoons brown sugar**
1/4 cup mushroom stock (see step 4)	**2 teaspoons salt**
1/4 cup sherry	**1 pound short tubular dried**
1/4 cup dark soy sauce	**pasta, such as penne rigate**

Serves 6

   1. Place a round cake rack in the bottom of a 4-quart deep, heavy enamel casserole with a tight-fitting cover.
   2. Remove the root end of the leek, then split the leek in half lengthwise all the way through. Place it under forcefully running warm water to remove all traces of sand. Cut the leek into 2-inch pieces. Place the leeks in the casserole on top of the rack.
   3. Rinse the pork shoulder under cold running water; then place it on top of the leeks, fat side down.
   4. Rinse the mushrooms. Place them in a bowl, then soak them in 1 cup cold water for 2 hours or until they are soft. Squeeze the mushrooms over the bowl. Clip off the stems with scissors. Quarter the mushroom caps. Place the stems and the water in which they were soaking in a small saucepan. Over low heat, reduce until 1/4 cup remains. Strain the mushroom stock into the casserole containing the pork.
   5. Place the casserole over high heat. Add the sherry, soy sauce, and ginger slices on top of the pork. Then add the chicken stock around the pork. Bring to a boil. Baste the pork a few times. Cover, then turn the heat to low, and simmer 2½ hours, checking every hour to see that the stock has not evaporated. The pork should cook at a slow simmer. Using two

spatulas, turn the pork over and simmer another 2 to 2½ hours. Baste the pork every so often and check to see that it does not stick and that there is an ample amount of stock left. Turn off the heat. As the pork will be quite tender at this point, place a spatula underneath the cake rack to prevent it from falling apart. Remove the pork (on the rack) from the casserole to a plate. Remove and discard the fat and the skin. Strain the sauce into a bowl and place the leeks and ginger onto the same plate as the pork. Defat the sauce, then return the pork (still on a rack), leeks, ginger, and sauce to the casserole.

6. Add the quartered mushrooms to the casserole containing the pork, along with the brown sugar. Simmer the pork without a cover over low heat until the sauce reduces to a thick, syrupy glaze. This will take about another ½ hour to 1 hour. During this final reduction, baste the pork occasionally. Turn off the heat.

WHEN READY TO SERVE

7. Bring a large kettle of salted water to a rolling boil. Add the pasta and cook until tender but firm. Drain in a colander.

8. Remove the cake rack from the casserole with two spatulas. With two wooden spoons or two pairs of chopsticks, tear the pork apart. Turn the heat to high. Add the drained pasta. Mix the pasta with the pork and the sauce for about 1 minute or until well combined. Serve immediately.

PLAN AHEAD

The entire recipe can be prepared two days ahead through step 6. Refrigerate. The pork only needs to be reheated and the pasta boiled at the last minute.

*NOTE

Shoulder of pork is also called fresh cali or picnic. As this cut has a thick bone running through it and skin on the outside, it is the most desirable cut to use. The best flavor will come from it. You can, however, substitute a loin of pork, in which case make sure it has the bone. I have also used an inexpensive cut of veal for this dish with success, either shoulder or the second cut of a rack of veal (which is going toward the neck).

Because of the high salt content in the soy sauce, use only salt-free Chicken Stock.

Chinese Pepper Pasta

This sauce is served on the Chinese fresh egg noodles called lo mein. Noodles are the staple of the North, as opposed to rice in all other parts of China. Besides being daily fare, they are also served on birthdays because the long length of the noodle symbolizes longevity.

2 tablespoons peanut oil
1 tablespoon minced garlic
1/3 cup scallions, white and green parts, cut into 1/8-inch rounds
2 tablespoons chopped cilantro leaves*
1 cup charred peppers, reserved from Spicy Pepper Salad*

2 tablespoons juice from Spicy Pepper Salad*
1 tablespoon Chicken Stock
1/2 teaspoon Hot Sauce*
1 tablespoon Oriental sesame oil

2 teaspoons salt
1/3 pound fresh lo mein*

Serves 2

1. In a 10-inch skillet, heat the peanut oil until it is hot but not smoking. Turn the heat to low and sauté the garlic and scallions until the garlic is lightly browned.

2. Add the cilantro and stir briefly. Add the charred peppers and the Spicy Pepper Salad juice. Continue to stir. Add the chicken stock and cook another minute. Add the Hot Sauce and sesame oil. Then turn off the heat.

WHEN READY TO SERVE

3. Bring a large kettle of salted water to a rolling boil. Add the fresh egg noodles. Cook 2 to 3 minutes. Drain in a colander.

4. Bring the sauce to a simmer. Add the drained pasta to the simmering sauce. With the heat on high, stir and toss 1 minute or until the sauce has been well combined with the pasta. Turn off the heat. Serve hot or at room temperature.

PLAN AHEAD

If you are planning to serve this Chinese Pepper Pasta at room temperature, you can make it early in the day. If you are planning to serve it hot, you can make the sauce early in the day, and you need only cook the pasta at the last minute.

*NOTE

Cilantro is also known as Chinese parsley or fresh coriander.

Chinese Pepper Pasta is a delicious and simple side pasta dish. However, it relies on one crucial ingredient that requires some advance preparation. You must make Spicy Pepper Salad and remember not to eat it all, as the recipe calls for 1 cup of the leftover salad. Because you will need 2 tablespoons juice from Spicy Pepper Salad, you must also save any settling juices.

For the Hot Sauce you can substitute ⅛ teaspoon Tabasco sauce.

If lo mein are not available, you can substitute an Italian fresh pasta.

Turkey Lo Mein

The skin from a leftover roast turkey is usually thrown out the next day because it has become soggy. What a mistake! Run it under the broiler. It is delicious—crisp like bacon and very flavorful. Turkey Lo Mein is a sensational recipe that uses this idea and also the leftover roast turkey meat. The only complaint I've had about the dish is that the recipe is more work than a Thanksgiving dinner.

1/3 cup Chinese mushrooms
2 cups shredded roast turkey skin
2 to 3 tablespoons rendered turkey fat (see step 2)

SEASONING SAUCE
1/4 cup dark soy sauce
2 tablespoons oyster sauce
1 cup combination turkey stock and drippings*

BINDER
1 tablespoon cornstarch dissolved in:
2 tablespoons medium-dry sherry

2 teaspoons salt
3/4 pound lo mein (thin fresh egg noodles)

2 medium leeks
1 cup mung bean sprouts
2 tablespoons rendered poultry fat*
2 cloves garlic, minced
1 tablespoon minced ginger
1 cup snow peas, strung and shredded
1 cup shredded unpeeled zucchini
1/2 medium-size red sweet pepper, shredded
1/2 medium-size yellow Holland pepper, shredded
3 cups shredded leftover roast turkey, combination light and dark meat

Serves 4–6

1. Rinse the mushrooms. Place the mushrooms in a bowl and then soak in water to cover for 1 hour or until they are soft. Squeeze the mushrooms over the bowl in which they were soaking. Clip the stems with a scissors and discard. Shred the mushrooms.

2. Preheat the oven to 350°. Place the turkey skin on an iron skillet and roast for 20 minutes or until the skin is as crisp as bacon. Pour the skin and the fat into a colander set over a bowl; allow to drain and cool. Reserve this rendered turkey fat for frying the noodles.

3. Turn the oven down to 250°. Combine the ingredients for the seasoning sauce.

4. Mix the binder.

5. Bring a large kettle of salted water to a rolling boil. Add the lo mein and cook 2 to 3 minutes. Drain the lo mein in a colander.

6. Remove the root end of the leeks, then split the leeks in half lengthwise all the way through. Place them under forcefully running warm water to remove all traces of sand. Shred the white and also the tender light green parts only (reserve the dark green part for basic Tomato Sauce or stock). The yield should be 1½ cups shredded leeks.

7. Place a wok over high heat for about 2 minutes or until it starts to smoke. Add the bean sprouts, shaking the wok occasionally. Cook until they scorch, then flip and cook on the other side. This whole procedure will take 2 to 3 minutes. Empty the bean sprouts onto a plate and reserve.

8. Return the wok to high heat for about 30 seconds. Add the reserved 2 to 3 tablespoons rendered turkey fat. After about 5 seconds it will be hot. Then add the noodles. Cook over high heat, shaking the wok occasionally. Flip the noodles and brown on the other side. This will take another minute or two. Transfer the noodles to a serving dish and keep warm in the preheated 250° oven. Do not wash the wok.

9. Add 2 tablespoons poultry fat to the wok and heat until hot but not smoking. Add the leeks and mushrooms; sauté over a low heat for about 2 minutes or until the leeks become limp.

Turn the heat to high; add the garlic and ginger. Stir a few seconds.

Add the snow peas, zucchini, red and yellow pepper. Continue to stir-fry over high heat for another minute.

Add the seasoning sauce and bring to a boil.

Restir the binder and add it to the wok all at once, continuing to toss. Add the shredded turkey, continuing to toss until the sauce thickens. Add the smoked bean sprouts. Turn off the heat. Mix well.

10. Place the turkey-and-vegetable mixture over the noodles.

Garnish with the turkey skin. Serve immediately.

PLAN AHEAD

All the preparations can be done early in the day for Turkey Lo Mein. Refrigerate.

*NOTE

For the turkey stock and drippings you can substitute Chicken Stock.

Rendered poultry fat can be purchased or made at home. For the 2 tablespoons of rendered poultry fat you can substitute an equal amount of peanut oil.

Lo Mein with
Braised Shiitake Mushrooms

3/4 **pound fresh shiitake**
mushrooms
1 1/2 **tablespoons peanut oil**
1 1/2 **tablespoons butter**
3 **tablespoons minced shallots**
1 **tablespoon dark soy sauce**
1 **teaspoon Hot Sauce***
1 **tablespoon oyster sauce**
1 **cup blanched broccoli**
florets

1/3 **cup red sweet pepper, cut**
in thin strips

2 **teaspoons salt**
1/3 **pound fresh lo mein (thin**
fresh egg noodles)*

2 **tablespoons peanut oil**

Serves 2–3

1. Using a mushroom brush, clean the mushrooms by rinsing briefly under cold running water. Remove and discard the stems. Cut the caps into thin strips.

2. In a wok or a 12-inch sauté skillet, heat the 1 1/2 tablespoons peanut oil and the butter until the butter foams. Add the shallots and sauté over a low heat for about 2 to 3 minutes or until lightly browned. Add the mushrooms and continue to sauté for another 10 minutes, stirring occasionally.

3. Stir in the soy sauce, Hot Sauce, and oyster sauce. Add the blanched broccoli florets and the red pepper, continuing to stir another 30 seconds. Turn off the heat.

WHEN READY TO SERVE

4. Bring a large kettle of salted water to a rolling boil. Add the lo mein and cook 2 to 3 minutes. Drain in a colander.

5. Place an iron skillet or a steel wok over high heat for about 2 minutes, or until it smokes. Add the remaining 2 tablespoons of peanut oil and heat until hot but not smoking. Make a noodle pancake by adding the noodles and allowing them to scorch on one side. Shake the pan occasionally. This will take about 2 minutes. Flip the noodles and let them scorch on the other side. Place the noodles on a flat serving dish.

6. Bring the sauce to a simmer and pour the sauce over the noodle pancake. Serve immediately.

*NOTE

For the Hot Sauce you can substitute 1/4 teaspoon Tabasco sauce.

If lo mein are not available, you can substitute an Italian fresh pasta.

Index

About the Authors

KAREN LEE is a nationally recognized authority on cuisine. She has supervised a highly successful catering business and cooking school since 1972. Her classes have received favorable editorial endorsements from the New York *Times, Bon Appétit, Cuisine, Food & Wine, House Beautiful, Better Homes and Gardens,* and *Travel & Leisure.* Her articles on food have appeared in the New York *Times Magazine, Food & Wine,* and *Working Woman.* She has made numerous appearances on radio and television throughout the country, and has given lecture demonstrations for retailers, cooking schools, and charitable organizations. Karen Lee has one son, Todd Hartman, who is attending college.

ALAXANDRA BRANYON, author of three off-Broadway plays, is the playwright/ lyricist half of Branyon/Kitchings, a song-writing team that has written numerous pop songs and two musical comedies, the latter of which received an award from the American Society of Composers, Authors, and Publishers. As a food writer, her articles have appeared in the New York *Times Magazine, Food & Wine,* and *Working Woman.* She co-authored *Chinese Cooking Secrets* (Doubleday, 1983) with Karen Lee.